STILL BREATHING

My Journey with Love, Loss,
and Reinvention

STILL BREATHING

MY JOURNEY WITH LOVE, LOSS, AND REINVENTION

KATIE JOY DUKE

NEW DEGREE PRESS

Note to the reader:
This memoir depicts actual events in the life of the author as truthfully as memory permits. Occasionally, dialogue consistent with the character or nature of the person speaking has been supplemented. All persons within are actual individuals; there are no composite characters. The names of some individuals have been changed to respect their privacy.

STILL BREATHING
My Journey with Love, Loss, and Reinvention
ISBN   979-8-88504-110-2 *Paperback*
          979-8-88504-737-1 *Kindle Ebook*
          979-8-88504-216-1 *Ebook*

For my daughters

Table of Contents

MY INSPIRATION

I was sitting alone in the quiet nursery reading a book on my Kindle. My eyes were swollen from crying, and my body was sore from giving birth. Eli and I had been home from the hospital for less than a week, and reality was beginning to sink in. Our baby was never coming home.

Poppy was dead, stillborn at full term. Nothing would ever be the same.

I looked up from my book and stared out the window of our three-story townhouse. The sky was wet and gray, typical for a November day in Seattle. I closed my eyes and remembered Poppy's sweet face. I'd always wonder what color eyes she had. I never imagined something so horrible could happen. How would I survive this devastation?

I was a childless mother, with empty arms and shattered dreams.

My focus shifted to the mother whose memoir I was reading. In *An Exact Replica of a Figment of My Imagination*, Elizabeth McCracken wrote about her first child, a baby boy named Pudding, who was stillborn at full term. Her story comforted my aching soul. *I wasn't alone.* Days into mourning, I related deeply to McCracken's heartbreak and her need to keep Pudding's memory alive.

As I sipped on warm chamomile tea that Eli, my husband, made me, I imagined writing my own story about loving and losing Poppy. The possibility that I, too, had a story to share sparked a flame in my spirit. I'd just begun to grieve, and already I was desperate to find connection by sharing my experience with others.

What would it look like to become a whole person again after my life felt ripped into a thousand pieces? How might Poppy's story make a difference in the lives of others? She had already transformed mine. I immediately started writing. I filled journals, took an online memoir writing class, and eventually started a blog. Writing gave me solace and helped me make sense of the pain and sadness that enveloped me as I existed without my daughter.

Before Poppy died, I had no clue stillbirth was so prevalent, but the Centers for Disease Control and Prevention reports that stillbirth affects one of every 160 pregnancies. Stillbirth is defined as a death at twenty weeks gestation or greater, and each year about 24,000 babies are stillborn in the United States alone. The Star Legacy Foundation reports that every year over 2.6 million stillbirths occur worldwide.

Poppy's death was unimaginable. Love and naivety carried us so far, and then what seemed like a sure thing was ripped away at the end. I heard it over and over in the early days of my grief: Losing a child is the worst thing that can happen to a person. I agree. It's an experience I wouldn't wish on anyone, but my grief was a catalyst for change and personal transformation. Because of my grief, I grew spiritually, learning how to be with pain and discomfort rather than turning away from or minimizing it. I learned to sit with the uncertainty of life and began living outside my comfort zone. Now, I am no longer afraid to talk about death, and

I've learned how to hold space and empathize with others in their grief and pain.

Poppy died in October 2015, and life was hard for quite some time. My rainbow baby, Moxie, was born two years later in October 2017. Pregnancy after loss was an act in faith and courage. Just as my dream of becoming a mother to a living child came true, my father's health rapidly declined, and he lost a long battle with prostate cancer on February 27, 2019.

Writing this book has helped me make sense of the things that happened, and even when I had no idea how I would make it through, I never gave up on the story. In *Rising Strong: How the Ability to Reset Transforms the Way We Live, Love, Parent, and Lead*, Brené Brown says, "Owning our story and loving ourselves through that process is the bravest thing we'll ever do. We own our stories so we don't spend our lives being defined by them or denying them. And while the journey is long and difficult at times, it is the path to living a more wholehearted life."

My path to healing was both long and winding. Now, in the wake of both birth and death, I own this story by choosing love over fear, acceptance over resistance, and being over doing.

If you have experienced miscarriage, stillbirth, or infant death, this book is for you. If you are missing a parent or loved one, this book is also for you. Perhaps someone you love is grieving and you want to help them, but you don't know how. Let this story guide your way. Even in our darkest moments, we are never alone. Join me on this journey of understanding and growth, as I open my heart, admit my fears, and learn to ask for help.

Grief is a messy process, and life after loss can feel impossible. Even when you don't feel it, there is hope. You have permission to slow down, unravel, and question everything. That's what I did, and I made it through.

Poppy taught me how to face the hardest things in life courageously. She taught me how to hold space with myself and others and how to talk about things that hurt without shame. She was a sacrifice, and she became my spirit guide.

I'll never know who I would have become had Poppy survived, but I do know I am proud of who I am now and how I've transformed because of my loss. My writing is a testament to the love I have for my daughters and my father. Sharing my story with the world is the most vulnerable and courageous act I've ever taken.

I hope Poppy finds a place in your heart. She'll forever be alive in mine.

PART I:

US

CHAPTER 1:

OUR SUNSET

———

Daylight peeked over the horizon. Roosters crowed, and I crawled out of bed to pee for the third time that night. My boyfriend, Eli, snoozed undisturbed in the king-size bed as I tiptoed down the stairs of the condo we were renting on the Hawaiian Island of Kauai.

Why do I need to pee again? I wondered. We'd arrived on the island the day before, and we were adjusting to the new environment and time zone, so I brushed off any concern and chalked it up to travel. We were on a tropical Hawaiian vacation in February of 2015. I'd long fantasized about taking a winter holiday like this one and now, as a successful lawyer in my mid-thirties, I was living out my dream with someone I adored.

Two weeks prior, Eli and I had moved in together in Seattle. I moved from my studio apartment in the trendy neighborhood of Capitol Hill to his three-story townhouse a few miles away in North Beacon Hill. I hoped this decision would be permanent. The only other time I'd lived with a boyfriend was out of convenience. That experience didn't end well, and I swore I'd never do it again. This time was for love. Eli was kind, attentive, funny, and driven—everything that mattered to me for a lasting partnership.

We'd dated for just over a year and decided the time was right to live together. I was thirty-four, Eli was thirty-seven, and we made a good team. I made (most of) the plans, and he happily went along. We knew what we wanted, and we wanted each other.

I had called my mom and dad on my last morning in my studio apartment, as I was packing up a few final things. They were my best friends, and I could always tell them what was going on in my heart.

"I'm nervous," I admitted. "Living with Eli is what I want, but it feels like the end of an era."

My dad, Jim, chuckled. "It is the end of something, Angel Pie, but it's also the start of something new. Eli is a great guy, and we support you." My dad's vote of confidence was encouraging, and he knew me well; I enjoyed change and always found ways to thrive.

I'd moved to Seattle two years earlier from New York City, where I'd landed my first job out of law school as a social justice attorney for a non-profit organization. I loved New York City, but after five years of pounding the proverbial pavement, I was ready for a different lifestyle. When an opportunity to move to Seattle presented itself, I jumped at the chance. I'd been praying for a fresh start, and the Universe gave it to me.

As I stumbled through the condo in Kauai, I was so glad I made the decision to move across the country. Everything was falling into place, and I'd never been more secure in myself. I used the bathroom and crawled back in bed next to Eli's warm body. He nuzzled into me, and I fell asleep again despite the noisy roosters outside.

Kauai is a very special island, and Eli and I were determined to enjoy as many adventures as possible. That afternoon we took a helicopter tour and saw extraordinary sights from the air—waterfalls, canyons, gorges, prehistoric cliffs, and the endless blue ocean. Neither one of us had ever flown in a helicopter before, and we were awestruck and zonked after the flight. Eli was mildly seasick, and I almost fell asleep in the car on the drive home. Rather than fight our exhaustion, we cuddled up and took a long afternoon nap back at our condo.

Valentine's was the next day, and I was feeling anxious. Was Eli going to propose? I couldn't stop thinking about it. We knew we were meant for one another; we had looked at engagement rings, and he'd received my dad's blessing. It was only a matter of time before he popped the question.

Valentine's morning, we ventured up to Turtle Beach on the North Shore, where the water was crystal clear and perfectly calm. We snorkeled with hundreds of tropical fish, and then I sunbathed while Eli relaxed in the shade. We got home from the beach around three in the afternoon and made a reservation at Duke's restaurant for dinner. I wore a simple black dress and tucked a red hibiscus flower behind my ear. When we got to the restaurant, my heart sank a little.

This restaurant was not the place to propose.

We sat down and ordered drinks before I excused myself and went to the ladies' room. I stood at the bathroom sink and looked myself square in the eyes. "Katie, let it go. You are on vacation with your lover in one of the most romantic places on Earth. It doesn't matter if he proposes on this trip. It will happen someday. From this moment on, no more thinking about it. Be present and enjoy the moment!" I winked at myself and straightened my hair before walking back to our table.

Eli had a big smile on his face as he held up a carved pineapple and took a sip of his pina colada. I picked up my Mai Tai and made a toast. "To us!" I cheered.

"To us!" he replied. We clinked our drinks and enjoyed a delicious dinner together.

The following morning while making breakfast, Eli suggested we find somewhere to watch the sunset that evening. "Great idea," I agreed. I wasn't used to him making the plans, but who would refuse a Hawaiian sunset?

We enjoyed a full day of snorkeling and swimming at Poipu Beach on the south end of Kauai, and keeping an eye on the sun, we sipped happy hour margaritas and ate tacos at a nearby restaurant afterward. Then we picked up a bottle of wine and sought out a spot to watch the sunset. As we cruised along Lawai Road, we noticed a grassy area that looked out over the Pacific Ocean. The lawn was adjacent to a fine dining restaurant called The Beach House, and knowing the sunset wasn't going to wait for us, we agreed it was a perfect spot to relax.

Picnic blanket spread, wine poured, and tropical breeze blowing, we snuggled into one another. As the sun approached the horizon, people poured out of the open-air restaurant. Families and lovers posed for pictures with the Hawaiian sun at their backs. My heart swelled with wonder and love. Little did I know Eli was sweating the unexpected company. The sun was fully beyond the horizon when I suggested we pack up and head home. Scrambling, Eli pointed up to the sky.

"See that little wisp of clouds?" he asked. "Let's watch and see if that changes color."

"Okay, why not?" I replied and poured more wine.

The sunset crowd dissipated, and we were relatively alone on our patch of grass. Eli turned toward me and told me he loved me. "I love you too, sweetie," I said. He leaned in and kissed me. Then he told me he loved me again and leaned in for more kisses.

"You're being weird," I giggled aloud. Then he propped up on one knee and reached into his pocket, pulling out a red velvet box. My heart started racing. Inside shone a beautiful diamond ring, and he reached for my left hand.

"Katie, you are the girl of my dreams. Will you make me the happiest man alive and spend the rest of your life with me as my wife?"

"Yes! Yes! Of course I will!" He pulled me in for a long, sweet kiss, and I melted in his arms.

Just like that, we were engaged.

CHAPTER 2:

OUR SURPRISE

———

Roosters be damned, I was not getting out of bed. My fiancé's body was so comfy. Fiancé! Oh, how I loved the sound of that. I held my brand-new engagement ring into the light streaming through the window above, wiggled my fingers, and watched sparkles bounced off the glittering stone.

I rolled on top of Eli and straddled his warm body. I looked into his sleepy eyes and smiled. "Let's have a yearlong engagement," I suggested.

"Okay, we'll talk about it," he chuckled.

I was in no rush to plan a wedding. I wanted to embrace life as Eli's fianceé. After a playful romp in the sheets, we made breakfast and packed up our backpacks with water and a picnic lunch. Swimsuits, snorkel gear, and hiking shoes were already in the car, and we were ready for whatever the day had in store.

That morning we drove to Waimea Canyon on the western side of Kauai where we would hike to Waipo'o Falls. The views outside my passenger seat window were lush and vibrant. I was so excited to be on another adventure with Eli. We turned off Highway 50 and started the long climb up Waimea Canyon Drive. The higher we drove, the cloudier it got, and I was concerned we might not see anything from the top. We pulled over at mile marker eighteen and joined other hopeful tourists waiting to catch a view of the island below. Just as we reached the guardrails at Kalalua Overlook, the clouds parted, and we saw amazing views of the Napali Coast spread out beneath us. I breathed in the warm tropical air and felt energized. It seemed like an auspicious beginning to our day.

On our way back down Waimea Canyon Drive, we pulled over at mile marker fourteen for our hike. We reached the bottom of the trail just around lunchtime and took in the beautiful sight of Waipo'o Falls. I couldn't wait to swim underneath a waterfall. A few people were swimming, but more were lounging on rocks in the sun or taking pictures. I stepped into the water to test the temperature and found that it was freezing.

I grew up a competitive swimmer, and I love a good challenge, so I wasn't going to let the temperature stop me from swimming to the waterfall. Eli, on the other hand, would need prodding. We agreed to picnic in the sun before taking the plunge. I devoured my sandwich while Eli ate more slowly; I think he was trying to buy time before I demanded that he join me in the water.

I decided I'd move things along and stood up to undress. I was in Hawaii, so I might as well work on my tan. The rock we picnicked on was huge and flat, and there was plenty of room to move about, but when I stood up and lifted my arms over my head, the world shifted, and I lost my balance for a moment. I took a deep breath and grounded myself.

Then a thought flashed across my mind. *Could I be pregnant?*

My cycle was a few days late, but I'd passed it off as a side effect of travel. *Maybe that's why I needed to pee in the middle of night?* Until that very moment, pregnancy hadn't crossed my mind. Now I was suspicious, but I didn't dare mention it to Eli.

"Let's do this babe! That waterfall is calling my name."

Eli reluctantly obliged, and in his defense, it was the coldest water I've ever swum in. We hollered and kicked until we reached the waterfall across the pool, where we crawled onto the rocks behind the raging water, and then, as lovers do, held each other and kissed. His soft lips were a balm to the chill on my skin. We swam back to the rock and warmed our bodies in the sun before hiking back up the canyon.

That evening, while picking at my dinner, I had an internal debate with myself. *How should I bring up my premonition to Eli?* We'd only been engaged for a day, and a pregnancy seemed awfully sudden. As we drove home toward our condo in Kapaa, my anxiety bubbled over. I couldn't avoid the conversation any longer.

I took a deep breath. "Hun." I looked over at him from the passenger seat. "I think we should stop at a drug store and grab a pregnancy test."

"What? Really?" he asked. He sounded excited.

"Yeah, I'm a couple days late, and this afternoon before we swam, I had this weird dizzy feeling when I stood up to take my clothes off. I'm kind of freaking out and can't stop thinking about it, so I'd just like to know for sure."

"Of course, honey! No problem. Let's do it." He turned his eyes back to the road, and I swear he did a little happy dance from the driver's seat.

When we got home, I made my way straight to the bathroom with the box of pregnancy tests. I read the instructions from start to finish—for best results, it said I should wait until the morning when hCG, the pregnancy hormone, would be the strongest. I couldn't wait that long. I sat down to pee, not bothering to close the door.

The stripe on the pregnancy test turned positive the moment my urine touched it. I looked at the instructions one more time and then stared at the results in disbelief.

"But we just got engaged," I moaned to myself. I felt numb. "It's positive, Eli," I uttered in his direction through the open bathroom door.

Eli looked up from the futon where he was sitting with his computer. His brown eyes sparkled, and a gigantic smile spread across his face. He was thrilled, no question in that. I joined him on the futon and cuddled into his shoulder. I didn't know how to feel.

Eli seemed totally okay with this surprise from the very beginning, and I credit him for helping me overcome my initial state of shock. We sat together for over an hour thinking through the turn of events. When did it happen? I studied the app where I tracked my cycles, and it became clear. I must have ovulated early the previous month when we thought it was safe to have unprotected sex. Classic.

We absolutely wanted to be parents, but it was something I wanted to plan. I was excited to be Eli's fianceé, then his wife, and *then* someday the mother of his children, but Eli's positive mindset and tender heart calmed my worried mind.

"Katie, I get it. This is fast and not what we expected, but what great timing, huh? I mean seriously. I proposed yesterday! That's amazing. I'm the luckiest guy on the planet. Thank goodness I finally got up the nerve to ask you!"

I looked at his kind face and couldn't help but feel joy. He wanted all of this—me and our child. It was a pure blessing.

"You're right." I smiled at the synchronicity. "Oh my god, you're right! This is amazing. We're going to be parents. I can't believe it. No, I have to believe it."

The night before, I had called family and friends to tell them Eli popped the question. Now I had a burning desire to tell someone I was pregnant too. Who would I entrust with this precious news? Althea, my best friend from law school.

"Mind if I call Althea, Eli? I've just got to tell somebody. This is too crazy to be true."

"Go for it honey."

Althea and I shared a wonderful conversation that evening. We'd been through thick and thin together including the birth of her son a few years prior. She helped me see the serendipity of the previous two days. "You're going to be an amazing mom, Katie," she encouraged me. "Plus, now we get to be mommies together!"

I took the second pregnancy test the following morning. Like the first, that test was also positive, and the joy of our good fortune was setting in, too.

CHAPTER 3:

OUR CELEBRATION

———

Everything changed the moment those pregnancy tests confirmed life was inside me. I was going to be a mother. One day I was obsessing about whether my boyfriend would propose, the next, he did, and the day after that we learned I was pregnant. It happened so fast.

Before leaving Kauai, Eli and I decided we'd marry at the end of my first trimester. So much for my yearlong engagement! We also nicknamed our baby Poppyseed thanks to a pregnancy app that compared our five-week-old fetus to the size of a poppy seed. We agreed to keep Poppyseed a secret from as many people as possible, but especially from our parents. We wanted to surprise them on our wedding night. That meant planning a wedding in eight weeks and hoping my baby bump wasn't obvious by the time I walked down the aisle.

We set the date for April 25, 2015. Initially, we planned an intimate ceremony for our parents only, but we changed our minds a few weeks before the event and invited our local friends too. We reserved Parson's Garden, a quaint park in Queen Anne, for the afternoon ceremony and prayed for sunshine. In lieu of a reception, we planned a champagne brunch at our townhouse for the following morning. It was unconventional, but Eli and I enjoyed bending the rules.

Our officiant was a warmhearted man with a powerful voice named Pastor Dave. He sent us a wealth of ideas on how to make our wedding memorable and unique to us as a couple. Eli and I were relaxing on the couch looking over vows and ceremony scripts Dave provided when I got a harebrained idea.

"Wouldn't it be funny if we asked Dave to begin the ceremony like the wedding scene in *The Princess Bride*?" I asked.

"Ooh, that would be hilarious. Do you think people would get it?" Eli asked.

"It's a cult classic. I'm sure they would. It doesn't matter anyway; we can do what we want," I said in a sassy tone.

A few weeks after we first met in November of 2013, Eli celebrated his thirty-sixth birthday. Our mutual friend Suz hosted a "movie night" birthday party for him, and we watched *The Princess Bride*. I'd seen the movie a hundred times, and it turned out we could both recite most of the script from memory. After that evening, *The Princess Bride* became our movie.

Back on the couch, we found the wedding scene on YouTube and watched together as evil Prince Humperdink forced helpless Princess Buttercup into wedlock. "Mawage is what bwings us togethah today," the stuffy priest proclaimed.

"Man and wife! Say man and wife!" Prince Humperdink demanded as the Dread Pirate Roberts threatened to bust down the door. Eli and I laughed until our stomachs hurt. We sent an email to Pastor Dave explaining our idea, and to our delight, he was on board.

The weather gods blessed us with sunshine the afternoon we wed. The dogwood trees in Parson's Garden dazzled with pink blooms, and a weeping willow covered in tiny green leaves swayed gently in the cool spring air. My flowers, hair, and makeup came together perfectly, and I wore Spanx to minimize my tiny baby bump. Although I was nervous my wedding gown would no longer fit, I was delighted I could still zip it over my expanding rib cage and bust line.

Our friend and wedding photographer, Jeff Shipley, took pictures of me and Eli for our "first look" in a quiet corner of the garden. Eli looked dapper in a tan seersucker suit, and I felt gorgeous in my empire-waist gown. I remember holding my flowers over my belly thinking about the little life secretly joining our celebration.

After our "first look," Pastor Dave pulled us aside for a few last-minute words of wisdom. We were giddy with anticipation. "Eli, when I say, 'You may kiss the bride,' make sure it's a long kiss. Really pull her in. I want to make sure I have enough time to step aside so Jeff gets a couple shots of just the two of you."

"No problem, Dave. That I can do," Eli replied.

"Alright then. We're all ready." Pastor Dave winked at us.

Eli and I gave each other one last kiss, then I walked with my dad, Jim, to the front entrance of the garden. We waited arm in arm until Sarah, our cellist, started playing Johann Sebastian Bach's "Sheep May Safely Graze." My dad escorted me down an aisle of cream-colored rose petals. It was an honor to have my dad's blessing and to know he loved the man I was marrying.

Over sixty friends and family stood on either side of the aisle, and everyone was smiling. Eli and I had an incredible community, and it was exhilarating to see everyone there to celebrate us. At the end of the aisle, my dad kissed me, and

I took my place with Eli in front of the crowd. Pastor Dave took a deep breath and began.

"Mawage!" Pastor Dave bellowed. He mastered the unmistakable drawl of Peter Cook's character from *The Princess Bride.* "Mawage is what bwings us togethah today. That blessed arrangement, that dream within a dream." Laughter rippled through the crowd as Eli squeezed my hands. The joke was a hit and set the stage for a lovely ceremony.

Next, our friend Rob read the passage "On Marriage" from *The Prophet* by Kahlil Gibran. My favorite line from the short poem was "Stand together yet not too near together: For the pillars of the temple stand apart, And the oak tree and the cypress grow not in each other's shadow." Eli and I chose that passage because we value ourselves as individuals who need freedom to grow within the promise of our love.

After exchanging our vows, Pastor Dave asked, "Who has the rings?" I gazed down the lawn toward Eloisa, my sister-in-law, and JD, my five-year-old nephew, who was our ring-bearer. Eloisa held up her arms in that universal "I don't know" fashion.

I looked over at Kirsten, my "honorary" maid of honor, who had been my dear friend since our freshman year in college. She'd helped me zip up my dress that morning and added finishing touches to my hair and makeup. On the drive to the ceremony, I handed her a bag with the wedding rings and instructions to give them to Eloisa.

Kirsten looked at me blankly. "The rings are in the pink Victoria's Secret bag I gave you on the drive over," I said.

"Oh, shoot. The bag is still in your dad's car," she apologized. I looked over at my dad, who reached into his pocket and tossed the car keys over the aisle to Kirsten. She ran off, and we were left to wait. Sarah, our cellist, started playing music.

I smiled and shrugged my shoulders at the snafu, then I turned to Pastor Dave and in my most demanding tone hollered, "Man and wife! Just say man and wife!"

Eli and Dave threw their heads back in laughter. It was the perfect diversion. Before we knew it, JD ran down the aisle with our wedding rings, and we proclaimed, "I do!"

After the ceremony when the marriage certificates were signed and the last guest hugged goodbye, Eli and I walked back to our car as husband and wife. We were eager to get home and relax before heading to the Willows Lodge where we would spend the night as newlyweds. Before getting into the car, Eli unhooked the back of my dress, and I wiggled out of the Spanx before sitting down. "Ah…" I let out a long sigh and let my belly relax for the first time in hours.

We giggled all the way home and reminisced about our perfect day. Eli carried me over the threshold, and I ran upstairs to the bathroom. He ate a bowl of cereal, and we smooched a little in the kitchen before grabbing our overnight bags. Our big announcement was only hours away, and I remember feeling grateful that we had the evening to surprise our parents over a fancy meal.

Eli and I checked into our room at the Willows Lodge in the heart of Woodinville. Our suite had a beautiful canopy bed and French patio doors overlooking a meadow of spring wildflowers. We had an hour to relax before dinner, so we made love.

We held hands as we walked next door to The Herb Farm for dinner. I was glowing. We were chatting with our parents in the restaurant's front lounge when I picked up a copy of *The Herb Farm Cookbook*. I flipped open the cover to the dedication page. It read, "For my mother, Poppy." I touched my belly, then got Eli's attention and showed him discreetly, to which he smiled and gave me a wink.

Before dinner, we toured The Herb Farm's gardens and learned about the chef's inspiration for our nine-course meal.

We couldn't wait to share Poppyseed with our parents, so after the first course, Eli placed a sealed envelope in front of each of our parents. Without saying more, we invited them to open their gift.

Each envelope contained a picture of Poppyseed's first ultrasound from earlier that month. She was lying on her back, and one of her legs stuck straight up. Although she was only twelve weeks gestation at the time, we knew we were having a girl because we'd opted for state-of-the-art blood work that distinguishes gender before ultrasound technology can.

My mom, Louise, looked at the photo, looked up at me, looked back at the photo, and burst into tears. My dad studied the photo as though he wasn't quite sure what he was looking at, and then let out a bellowing laugh and huge grin. "Oh Katie Joy, Eli, this is wonderful news." Eli's stepmother Janice threw her hands up in the air, and John, my father-in-law, chuckled with grandfatherly pride. Overcome with relief, I let out a huge sigh. No more holding in. We were having a baby, and it was time to celebrate.

Eli and I checked out of our hotel the next morning after a wonderful night's sleep and looked forward to seeing our wedding guests once more for brunch. We were excited to make our final surprise announcement to our friends. Our parents and a few good friends were preparing the food when we arrived, and I got to work putting the finishing touches on the chocolate raspberry wedding cake I'd made in advance of the occasion.

Our 1,100-square-foot house was packed that afternoon, and the energy was magical; no one seemed to mind the close quarters. The mimosas flowed, and the conversation was jovial. After decorating the cake, I invited Eli to join me in our tiny downstairs bathroom for a quick chat. I locked the door and asked him how we were going to announce the baby. I was more nervous than I'd been at dinner the night before, so we crafted a quick plan and shared a nice long kiss.

After mingling with our guests, we invited everyone to the main floor of the townhouse for a toast. As they gathered, my dad entertained the crowd with a story about the day Eli asked for my hand in marriage. It was the previous October, and he and my mom were visiting Seattle from their home in Thomasville, Georgia. I was still living in my studio apartment at the time, and Kirsten and my mom were helping me make dinner when my dad announced he was going to the rooftop to smoke. Eli asked to join him.

While they were together, Eli asked my father for his blessing. Apparently, my dad didn't know how to respond or what to say, and both men were a bit out of sorts when they came back to the apartment. We were just about to serve dinner when Eli and my dad sat down on opposite ends of the couch.

"Something happened while Eli and I were upstairs," my dad started. I turned around from the stove and looked at my dad. "Eli asked me if he could marry Katie." My heart skipped a beat, and all the air left the room. Daddy looked at me and asked, "Katie, do you want to marry Eli?"

My mom covered her mouth in horror. "Jim! Jim!" she exclaimed. "What are you doing?"

I let out an awkward giggle. "Well, Dad, I think that's a question I'll let Eli ask me when he's ready. Know what I mean?"

My dad froze when he realized his faux pas. "I'm sorry everyone. You're right, Katie." He looked over at Eli, dumbfounded. "Eli, I wasn't expecting this. I—I didn't mean to do that. I'm going to stop talking now."

"Good idea, Daddy!" I said. "Okay everybody; dinner's ready. Let's eat some curry and forget about it, shall we?" I turned back around to the stove and prayed my appetite would return.

Listening to my dad retell the story at our wedding brunch was almost as nerve wracking as the actual experience, but I had a good laugh because everything worked out and my dad lived to tell the tale. He congratulated us both with a hug and a kiss and turned the floor over to John, my father-in-law.

John is an excellent storyteller—even if he tells the same stories again and again—but this story I'd never heard. He started by describing Eli as a caring, thoughtful, and strategic man. Then, he took us back to a phone call he had with Eli the summer before we met.

"Eli was at one of those Burning Man parties you all go to, and he mentioned that he'd 'seen a girl,'" John snickered. "I asked him if he'd 'talked to the girl' and he said, 'No, she was with someone.'"

I blushed and looked at my husband who was sitting by my side. "Really?" I whispered with a smile. Eli squeezed my hand and nodded. I remembered that party well. It was an annual fundraiser in Seattle for a group who camped together in Nevada at the annual Burning Man event. I was dating someone at the time, but that relationship wasn't going anywhere.

John went on to share that he encouraged Eli to be patient. If it was meant to be, he'd run into me again. "Eli's patience paid off when he met Katie at a different party three months later. Clearly, it was meant to be." John raised his glass and looked at me. "To the perfect girl for my son." My heart swelled as he leaned in for a kiss.

With our fathers' speeches behind us, Eli and I stood up to address our friends and family. Eli recounted the evening he proposed and how throngs of people descended upon the restaurant lawn just as he was about to pop the question.

"I wanted to propose on our vacation, but I didn't want to do it on Valentine's Day because that felt cheesy. By the next morning, the ring was burning a hole in my pocket, and I couldn't wait another day. So that night, I proposed after the last wisp of a cloud turned pink. And she said, 'Yes!'" He turned to me to let me finish the story.

"So, the next morning when I woke up, after staring at my shiny diamond ring, the first thought I had was I wanted a yearlong engagement. No need to rush anything, right? That afternoon we hiked to a waterfall, and I had this funny feeling just as we were about to go swimming that something was a little off. That night as we were driving home from our adventurous day, I suggested we stop at the drug store to grab a pregnancy test." I paused to let that detail sink in with the crowd.

Then, Eli and I threw our hands up and recited in unison: "That night we found out we were having a baby!"

I'd never seen so many shocked and happy faces at the same time. The room erupted in celebration as Eli and I embraced. Oh, the relief. For ten weeks, we'd held this secret close to our hearts. Finally, Poppyseed and our immense love for her could be known.

CHAPTER 4:

MY GOLDEN PREGNANCY

I loved being pregnant. I was one of those women who glowed, and my radiance bubbled from the inside out. With the wedding behind us and our baby no longer a secret, I fully embraced the transformation into motherhood. Eli was equally excited for fatherhood. The promise of parenthood magnified our newlywed romance and strengthened our bond as a team.

Eli and I took weekly "baby bump" pictures to keep track of my expanding belly. I wore the same hot pink booty shorts and tie-dyed tube top for each picture, and I loved comparing my body to the previous week's pictures. I got a strange thrill watching my body change shape, and I couldn't wait for my bump to be more obvious. I'd hidden my pregnancy for the first trimester, and now I wanted everyone to know about the miracle happening within me.

In mid-May, we flew to the Big Island of Hawaii for an unexpected honeymoon. We hadn't planned a honeymoon, but my boss Omar surprised me by assigning three disability claims to argue in the capital city of Hilo. I was working full time as a Social Security disability attorney and traveled for work on a regular basis. My territory covered Washington, Idaho, Utah, Montana, Alaska, and when I was lucky, Hawaii.

For our honeymoon, Eli and I celebrated with a three-night vacation at the Four Seasons Resort on the Kona Side of the island. My sister, Kellee, and I were chatting on the phone about our last-minute opportunity to vacation, and she encouraged us to splurge. "You only get one honeymoon, Katie. And with the baby coming soon, you won't regret it."

We basked in tropical luxury. Poolside piña coladas (virgin for me), steak and sushi dinners, and room service crème brûlée. We swam in saltwater pools, went stand-up paddle boarding at the beach, and watched the sunset from lounge chairs nestled in the sand. One morning, I left Eli sleeping in bed and walked out to the ocean to enjoy the early morning alone. Cross-legged in the sand, I meditated and connected with the growing life inside me. Everything felt easy and intuitive.

For the first time in my adult life, I had purpose and value beyond my intellect. I was a perfectionist with high expectations for myself; I got straight A's throughout school and graduated college with highest honors. I tackled law school immediately thereafter and was an attorney in New York City at twenty-seven years old. I worked hard to accomplish and achieve, always comparing myself to women ten years my senior. Despite the accolades, the good job, and the salary, I struggled with feelings that I was never enough. But pregnancy was different; I didn't have to think my way through it. My body knew what to do. I was amazed by the profound process occurring naturally within me.

Home from our honeymoon, we had another routine ultrasound. Poppyseed was meeting every growth milestone. We loved our midwives at the Swedish Midwifery Clinic in Ballard and felt protected in their care. We joined a pregnancy group at the clinic as well and built a supportive community with other first-time parents expecting babies in October. After our monthly group meetings, we'd go out for dinner with the other couples to learn about each other. We always had something to talk about: the latest awkward pregnancy symptom, putting together a registry, or planning a baby shower. We dreamed about the babies we'd soon be nursing and taking care of. It started to feel like a real community.

Poppyseed and I were happy together, and she was easy on me. I never had morning sickness, and I didn't have any crazy cravings. I also didn't mind answering personal questions from strangers, and I was more than willing to let them touch my belly if they asked. Whenever the opportunity arose, I'd share the romantic events that unfolded for me and Eli—our Hawaiian engagement, surprise pregnancy, charming wedding, and blissful honeymoon. The first time I felt Poppy move, I was lying on a massage table telling the massage therapist our love story. At first, I thought my tummy was rumbling with hunger, then I realized it was my baby wiggling around. It was magical. My life was a fairytale; how did I get so lucky?

Over the fourth of July, Eli and I joined a group of friends for a nineteen-mile, three-day trek through the Seven Lakes Basin in Olympic National Park. I couldn't bear the thought of missing out just because I was pregnant. My backpack weighed thirty pounds, and the strap barely snapped under my baby bump. There were exhausting moments when I didn't think I could take another step; then we'd reach a lookout where the view stretched for miles, and it was all worth it again.

Sleeping on the ground was grueling, something I swore I'd never do again while pregnant. Each night, I crawled out of our tiny tent and stumbled into the bushes to relieve myself. Squatting in the dark, I rubbed my belly and imagined the good times we'd have together. "Hello Poppyseed, my love. Are you ready for an adventurous life with me? You better get ready because it's going to be fun."

By August, we agreed that Poppy would be our daughter's first name. Although we debated over Clementine, Autumn, Margot, and Gwendolyn, Poppy was an obvious winner. I'd never known anyone named Poppy. It was a unique and memorable name that she'd practically chosen from the start.

For our "Baby Moon" and my thirty-fifth birthday, Eli and I took a ferry from Seattle to Victoria, British Columbia, and stayed the weekend at the Fairmont Empress, a chateau-style hotel built in 1908. We nibbled on cucumber sandwiches, petit fours, and scones with clotted cream at the hotel's famous High Tea. We talked in hoity-toity accents and sipped tea with our pinkies up. I relished every moment alone with Eli, but I couldn't stop imagining what life would be like with our little girl.

Would she come on time? What would delivery be like? Would I want to return to work after my three-month maternity leave? Would it be hard to lose the baby weight after she was born? I had so many questions, and all I could do was patiently await her arrival.

CHAPTER 5:

READY AND WAITING

———

Poppy was due October 25, 2015. One of the last items on my to-do list was arranging for a breast pump with my insurance company. When I was twenty-one years old, I had breast reduction surgery, a decision I'd never regretted, but it was likely that structural damage from the reduction would impact milk production or the flow of milk from my breasts. I was a breastfed baby, and although I don't remember breastfeeding itself, I could recall the intimacy my mom and I shared during that time. I wanted to create that with my baby too.

Not leaving anything to chance, I consulted with a lactation nurse named Lauren from the Lytle Center at Swedish Hospital in early October. After examining the scar tissue from my reduction as well as the structure of my breasts, Lauren prescribed a hospital-grade double breast pump and gave me resources from Stanford University on how to hand express breast milk. She explained that hand expression helped increase milk production and flow from the day a baby was born. Lauren assured me that I would have access to support if my milk production was low or if Poppy had trouble latching. I left the appointment feeling optimistic that my daughter would be a breastfed baby.

Next, I sought out a supplier for the pump and made an appointment with Nurturing Expressions in West Seattle. Kristen, the bright-eyed receptionist, told me someone from Nurturing Expressions would bring the pump to the hospital or to my home after Poppy was born. She filed my insurance paperwork, and we chatted about the beautiful baby I'd soon be holding in my arms.

As we talked, I noticed a poster behind Kristen's desk of a mother nursing her infant and the query "Does your cup runneth over? Consider donating your milk." It was an advertisement for the Northwest Mothers Milk Bank. *How interesting*, I thought to myself. I didn't know human milk banks existed, and it had never crossed my mind that some women produced more milk than their baby needed. It seemed like a good problem to have, my deepest worry being that I wouldn't make enough.

That afternoon, as I drove back over the West Seattle bridge toward home, I mentally scanned my to-do list and realized everything was crossed off. I took a deep breath and acknowledged myself for getting it all done. I was still glowing, but I was also getting quite uncomfortable. Sleep was difficult, my lower back was sore, and I was anxious about whether Poppy would arrive on time.

At our final prenatal appointment, Eli and I followed the routine of taking my blood pressure, weighing in, and listening to Poppy's heartbeat with one of the midwives. Our midwife asked Eli if he wanted to listen to Poppy's heartbeat through a Pinard Stethoscope, which looked rudimentary and reminded me of a bicycle bell without the honking part. We were used to hearing the *whoosh whoosh* sound of her magnified heartbeat through the electronic Doppler monitor.

The midwife showed Eli how to place the flat edge on my belly, and he held his ear against the open side to listen.

"Ah! There it is! We can't wait to meet you, little one." He smiled. It was always comforting to hear her heartbeat. We thanked our midwife, and she wished us luck before we joined the rest of our pregnancy group in the main meeting area.

The room was full of seven newborn babies and many exhausted new parents. Eli and I congratulated our friends as each couple shared the highlights and challenges of their birth stories. I was happy for them but envious too. This was the group's last official gathering, and as the only pregnant person remaining, I felt left out of the celebration.

I shared my disappointment with Eli on the drive home, and he assured me we'd be getting together with them soon enough. "Try not to worry about it, hun." He grabbed my left hand and rubbed it softly. "You've got the rest of your life to get together with those moms. Plus, think of all the tips and tricks they'll be able to share with you after Poppy gets here."

"You're right, Eli. I'm just so ready to meet her." I smiled and rubbed my round belly with my right hand. Poppy responded with a little kick, and I immediately felt better.

Poppy's due date arrived: Sunday, October 25. I woke up that morning feeling unsettled. I'd had a dream that Poppy was in danger. Her movements had slowed down, and when I scoured the internet and looked it up in my pregnancy book, everything suggested that was normal. I was exactly forty weeks pregnant, and she didn't have a lot of room to move around in there. I needed a way to calm my nerves, so Eli and I drove to Pike Place Market for a walk. I started to relax as we wandered among the flower stands and vegetable stalls.

We passed by a mom feeding her toddler a snack, and I commented in her direction, "Today is my due date!"

"Congrats," she cheered as she spooned yogurt into her son's mouth. "Walking yourself into labor, huh?"

"Yes, I'm trying!" I laughed in response.

Eli and I shared a light lunch and sat for a long while on a park bench overlooking the Puget Sound. I snapped a photo of the two of us and posted it on Facebook. By mid-afternoon I was having mild cramps low in my belly, and we drove home so I could rest. Eli and I wondered if the cramps were early contractions, but as first timers, it was hard to know. I was happy to lie down when we got home, and I fell asleep easily.

I woke up from my nap later that afternoon and my cramps were still there, but they weren't very painful. We met our friends Emma and Brandon at their place for dinner. An excellent cook and considerate friend, Emma made spicy chili hoping to get my labor started. I was exhausted when we got home again around nine and decided to go to bed. Just in case, I peeked inside my closet and looked through my hospital bag; everything was packed and ready to go.

I walked downstairs to wish Eli goodnight. A night owl, he was sitting on the couch with his computer. My cramps had grown a little stronger since dinnertime, and although I wasn't sure if they were contractions, I told him I didn't think I'd sleep through the night. He walked me upstairs and tucked me in with a kiss. Before going to sleep, I sent Robin, my doula, a text message letting her know how I was feeling, and I fell asleep around 10:30 p.m.

I woke up at 12:30 a.m. There was no denying it. I was in labor.

I hobbled downstairs, where Eli was still awake on the couch. I told him if he ever wanted to sleep again, he'd better go upstairs immediately. He went into a frenzy. I helped him calm down and asked him to grab my yoga ball from the garage.

"Are you sure you don't want me to stay awake with you?" he asked.

"No honey, please go get some sleep. You're going to need it. We don't need you sleep deprived before she's even born."

"Want to put on a movie or something?" he asked. I thought for a moment, and *Dumb and Dumber* popped into my head. We rented it on Amazon, and he went upstairs to rest. The movie sped by as my contractions got longer and stronger. The remote control stopped working, and I couldn't pause the movie when I was having a big contraction. A child of the '90s, I grew up on Jim Carrey's slapstick comedy, and sadly, I missed most of the funny parts.

Around 3 a.m., I decided to call Robin. She picked up on the first ring. I told her that my contractions were getting strong, and she told me to call my midwives. She warned me it could be several hours before we needed to go to the hospital. The midwife on call encouraged me to breathe and reminded me to stay at home until my contractions were consistently a minute long and four or five minutes apart. Meanwhile, Eli snoozed. I tried finding something else to watch on TV but ditched it in favor of concentrating on my breath and feeling through the pain.

I lost track of time.

I needed Eli, but I was in no shape to walk up the stairs, so I called him on the phone and heard it ring upstairs. He never picked up but was at my side in a flash. He was a hot mess. I loved him for it. Labor was intensifying, and I didn't think I could manage a phone conversation, so Eli called the midwives and Robin again. My contractions were coming in the 5-1-1 pattern we'd learned about in birthing class. For over one hour my contractions were coming every five minutes and were lasting one minute each. We got the green light to head to the hospital.

It was 4:30 a.m. when we got in the car. The moon was almost full, and my heart was bursting. To harness extra strength, I wore my grandmother's diamond-studded earrings and a beaded bracelet my mom gave me on my wedding day. I felt beautiful and extremely uncomfortable.

Our time had arrived.

PART II:

POPPY

CHAPTER 6:

THE HOSPITAL

———

We arrived at the hospital around 5 a.m. The streets were quiet, and our drive was easy except for my contractions, which kept coming at a steady pace. The sky was still black when we pulled into the patient drop off. I was wearing my favorite maternity skirt, a cozy sweater, and slip-on shoes. After checking in downstairs, an attendant pushed me in a wheelchair up to the birthing center while Eli parked the car. The elevator doors opened to the crescent-shaped nurses' station. I'd been there before on a tour with my pregnancy group, and it felt familiar and welcoming.

I was ready for a marathon. I had trained for months, and this was the official starting line.

The attendant wheeled me into my birthing suite, and a nurse greeted me warmly, introducing herself as Ann. Eli arrived a few minutes later with our bags and pillows. Ann asked if I wanted to wear a hospital gown or something of my own, and I dug into my bag for my gray-and-white-striped maternity robe. I stopped for a moment to breathe through a contraction. At the end of the contraction, I stepped out of my clothes and tied the short robe around my belly.

When Ann saw my legs in the maternity robe, she complimented me. "Oh good. You are obviously strong and healthy," she said.

I smiled at her compliment. "Yes, thanks. I do feel strong, and *very* ready for this baby to be here!"

Ann told us she was going to monitor the baby's heartbeat for twenty minutes to see how she was responding to my contractions. Ann asked if we had chosen a name, and I said yes, but stopped there. I thought we'd keep Poppy's name a surprise until she was born. Ann balked at my silence, and I looked over at Eli for his reaction. He shrugged his shoulders as if to say, "Why not?" so I proudly announced, "Her name is Poppy Annabelle Muir."

"What a lovely name," Ann replied. I looked down at my round, tan belly and smiled. Then I looked up at Eli and gave him a wink.

Ann asked me to sit on the edge of the bed as she turned on a doppler monitor to listen to Poppy's heartbeat. Poppy had been head down for a few months now, and her heartbeat was easy to find just below and to the left of my belly button. Ann squirted jelly onto the monitor and rubbed it over my belly.

She moved the monitor around a bit. She moved it around a bit more. "Where are you, baby?" she murmured to herself.

That's strange, I thought. I furrowed my brow and looked over at Eli sitting on the daybed. He looked worried, his shoulders tense. Ann set down the monitor and said she needed to get the midwife. "I'm having a hard time finding the heartbeat." She stepped out.

Eli and I sat in silence while I stared down at my tummy.

Ann returned almost immediately with Mia, one of the midwives we knew well from our pregnancy group.

"Hi, Katie. Hi, Eli." Mia nodded to us both. She picked up the doppler and placed it on my belly. The room was silent. She searched for Poppy's heartbeat while Ann stood at her side.

Mia took a deep breath and looked at me. "I'm sorry Katie, but we can't find a heartbeat."

Everything stopped.

Her words echoed inside my head. *We can't find a heartbeat.*

I looked over at my husband, whose face was in his hands. He was grasping what I couldn't fathom. "Eli?" I asked in desperation. "Eli? What are they talking about? What does this mean?" He started weeping. The jelly on my bare belly started to dry, and a chill passed through my entire body. He stood up and came over to me.

"She's dead?" I asked in disbelief. I looked at Mia and Ann, who stood motionless, their faces sunken. Then Mia nodded her head in confirmation.

I went numb.

Eli collapsed next to me and buried his head into my chest, wrapping his arms around my belly.

"She's dead?" I asked again. Except this time, I was wailing.

Much of what happened next is a blur. Eli held me, and we wept together. Ann and Mia retrieved a medical doctor who confirmed the inconceivable nightmare with an ultrasound machine.

There is a lot I don't remember about our thirty-six hours in the hospital, much of it erased by my own need to survive. The shock was overwhelming, the truth excruciating. Poppy had died inside of me. No one prepared us for that possibility. No book, no medical professional. No one.

As darkness closed in on my dreams, I asked Mia if they would have to cut Poppy out of me.

Mia coached me tenderly. "No, Katie. You'll want to give birth vaginally. Your body doesn't know that Poppy is gone. We would only perform a cesarean if it was necessary to protect your life." That made perfect sense, but I wasn't thinking clearly.

When did Poppy's heart stop beating?

I started shaking. I felt it in my bones. It was frightening. Uncontrollable, like a bad acid trip. I wondered if the shaking would ever stop. Would I be like this forever? Tunnel vision. No hope. I tried breathing to minimize the tremors, but that made my jaw quiver.

My doula, Robin, arrived at the hospital shortly after we learned the horrible news. We had become dear friends over the course of my pregnancy, sharing many long walks in Greenlake Park together and fantasizing about my future as a mother. She had two grown children, and motherhood was her life's joy. Robin wasn't prepared for our loss either, but she harnessed strength and helped us make difficult decisions.

Contractions came at random intervals. My body was still trying to do its job, and the pain was soul crushing.

"Robin, I want an epidural." She held my hand at the side of the bed. My body kept shaking. "I want narcotics too. Please help me," I cried. None of this was in my plan, but I couldn't bear to feel the contractions anymore. Robin consulted with Mia, and they agreed a small dose of fentanyl would ease the shaking and calm my spiraling mind.

Ann placed an IV port in my right arm for the narcotics, and an anesthesiologist administered the epidural in my back with the biggest needle I'd ever seen. Afterward, I lay back onto the hospital bed and closed my eyes. The hospital room and the hushed movements of people around me dissolved as the fentanyl seeped into my bloodstream.

As I drifted away from my hospital bed, my mind conjured images of the Milky Way. The stars and spirals and mystical nothingness of deep space swirled behind my eyelids. My heart, shattered in a million pieces, was splattered among the stars. In that infinite nothingness, I saw Poppy's soul. She was safe and off on another mission. Something in me knew I would survive.

I fell asleep for a little while and woke up in a fog. I lay there practically paralyzed and then moved my hands to my swollen breasts. What would happen to my breast milk? I remembered the poster at Nurturing Expressions advertising the Northwest Mothers Milk Bank.

Ann walked over with a cold washcloth. She dabbed it gently on my forehead, and I leaned toward her with my eyes still closed, asking her if I could donate my breast milk.

She took a moment to respond and then replied, "Yes, Katie, you can."

"Will you help me make that happen?"

"Yes, dear, we will." A glimmer of hope.

Mia checked my cervix shortly thereafter. I was only three centimeters dilated. My heart sank. Three centimeters was nothing. I needed to be fully dilated at ten centimeters to push. There was no telling when I'd get there. I couldn't feel my contractions anymore, but the nurses assured me they were still coming.

We decided to use a drug called misoprostol to help ripen my cervix. After placing the medicine on my cervix, Mia told me it could take upward of twenty-four hours to fully ripen. These medical interventions were a slap in my face. Nothing was going to bring Poppy's heartbeat back.

My womb had become a tomb.

I fell asleep again after learning it could take forever to become fully dilated, but sleep was fitful this time. The narcotics were wearing off, and I could hear everyone talking around me. My friend Emma's soothing voice stood out among the others, and I whispered her name in hopes she would hear me. Eli and I had prearranged for Emma to take pictures when Poppy was born, and Eli had called her at some point that morning after learning that Poppy was gone. She rushed over to my bedside. "Hello, sweet friend." Emma stroked my hair, and we looked at one another in dismay. Words escaped us both.

"I'm glad you're here, Emma."

"Me too. I'm so sorry, Katie."

"I know," was all I could say.

"Why don't you try to get more sleep? Eli and I are going to make some phone calls and let your family know what's going on."

My family. Shit. Everyone needed to know. "Thank you, Emma," I said before closing my eyes again.

I managed to sleep for another hour or so and woke up crying. Poppy was dead, and I had still to give birth. Eli came over to the bed and kissed my cheeks. "Would you like to talk with your parents?" he asked. "They know about Poppy, and they want to hear your voice."

"Sure, I guess."

I remember hearing their stunned voices and the sound of their tears, but I have no recollection of what they said. What could anyone say? My sister, Kellee, recalled later how eerily calm I seemed when she spoke with me over the phone.

How could this happen? We all wanted to know. Wiping away the tears, I swore we'd try to have another baby as soon as possible. My first child wasn't even born, and already I felt like I had to replace her.

A new nurse named Karen brought me a clipboard with a milk donation application attached from the Northwest Mothers Milk Bank. The narcotics had worn off, and I was coherent, if not numb. The application wanted to know everything about me from my medical history to my current lifestyle. The straight-A student in me sat up in bed and started filling out the application. I answered each question thoughtfully. It was good to focus on something other than our tragedy.

Megan, the midwife then on call, checked my cervix again around 3 p.m. To everyone's surprise, I was fully dilated. Poppy was ready to be born. Robin suggested I take off my bra so Poppy could rest on my bare chest when she was born. Someone lowered the lights, and several nurses prepared the room for delivery. A spotlight shined down from the ceiling between my legs.

I was lying on my back in the bed, propped up on a few pillows. Emma stood at my right, and Robin was on my left. Robin's husband, who came to support Eli earlier in the day, offered to take photos with Emma's camera when Poppy was born. We said yes. Eli stood at the head of the bed next to my face, close enough to whisper encouraging words into my ears.

Megan watched my contractions on a monitor and told me when I could push. She gave me a little Pitocin to get my contractions closer and stronger, but I couldn't feel any pain. My water broke, wetting the sheets beneath me. As I reached the end of the next contraction, I rounded my pelvis and pushed with all my might. I was numb from the epidural and couldn't gauge my progress, but Megan was encouraging.

"You're doing an excellent job, Katie. One more push, and she'll be here." Eli stroked my hair and kissed my forehead. We waited for the next contraction. I took a deep breath. One final push.

I felt a release as Poppy's body departed mine. I heard quiet gasps as Megan caught her body.

There is a black-and-white photograph of Eli and me smiling at one another the moment after Poppy arrived. We did it. Our baby was here.

And she was gone.

Our fairytale came to a tragic end.

CHAPTER 7:

POPPY

———

Poppy arrived at 3:39 p.m. on October 26, 2015.

Megan placed her on my chest, skin on skin, and Eli cut her umbilical cord. We covered her in a swaddling blanket and gently wiped off her skin. Her eyes were closed, and she didn't make a sound. Her skin was pale, almost translucent, though it was still warm from being inside my body.

Eli and I looked at her resting on my bare chest, and our tears flowed. The room was quiet as everyone gave us time to be with our newborn. I could hear the camera shutter opening and closing.

I held her tiny hand, her fingers were long and elegant, and her lips were full like mine. I told her how much I loved her, and my tears fell onto her skin. Eli rummaged through my hospital bag and found a crocheted hat I'd brought from home. It was too big, but we made it work. I wanted to keep her warm. I gazed upon her sweet face and cradled her perfect body, feeling joy and devastation all at once. Poppy was a beautiful baby.

The nurses asked us if we wanted her measurements, and of course we did. After cuddling with her for a while, Eli carried Poppy over to the scale where a nurse weighed and measured her. She was 7 pounds, 11.8 ounces and 20 inches long. We took her footprints too; she didn't squirm or make a fuss. First the left foot, then the right. We were making memories; the only ones we would have.

We made a lot of difficult decisions that day. My only regret is that I didn't give her a bath. Her skin was deteriorating, and there were little blisters on her arms, legs, and feet. I never asked anyone to explain exactly why the blisters were there, afraid the answer was too morbid. I couldn't bear the thought of tearing or injuring her skin while bathing her, so we left it alone and kept her wrapped in a blanket.

What can I say about the handful of hours I had with my firstborn? Precious. Sacred. Fleeting. The pain was immense as I merely prayed for my next breath to come.

How would I ever survive?

I made a promise to Eli that we would try again as soon as possible. I had no idea what I was promising. I was grasping at hope. He kissed my tears, nodded his head, and looked at me with the same resolve. "Yes, my darling. We can try again. Let's just be here now with Poppy while we can. I'd like to hold her for a little while."

Eli sat down and took his shirt off so they could be skin to skin. Robin took Poppy from my arms and carried her over to Eli. He held out his arms to cradle his child. He was a wonderful father.

Within the hour, a lactation nurse named Amy came by to meet us. She'd heard I wanted to donate my milk. Amy and I talked about the mechanics of hand expression, and what I should expect. Thankfully, I'd studied the videos given to me by the lactation consultant from the Lytle Center, and I wasn't learning about hand expression for the first time.

"Right now, you will be producing colostrum. There is no milk. You may be surprised at how little there is, but it's a precious fluid. Powerful. Made just for your baby by you." We met eyes. Mine were full of tears. "I'm so sorry, Katie. I know this is painful. What you're doing is honorable."

I can do this, I thought to myself. "This is important, Amy," I said aloud. "Poppy would want me to share."

"Are you ready to try?"

I nodded.

Amy sat with me as I expressed colostrum out of my breasts drop by drop. We collected the liquid gold onto a plastic teaspoon and sucked it up into a tiny syringe. Even in my devastation, every drop I collected gave me a tiny hint of joy. Oxytocin, the love hormone, coursed through me. I held Poppy in my lap while I expressed. I rubbed her tiny lips with some colostrum. It was hers after all.

I thanked Amy for helping me and let everyone know I was feeling tired. She said goodbye and promised she'd visit again. I wanted to close my eyes, but first I wanted to take a shower. Robin helped me out of the hospital bed for the first time in several hours. Bright red blood dripped from between my legs onto the floor. Lochia. Like all mothers, I would bleed for a few weeks as my body healed from giving birth.

I sat down on the toilet and cried into my hands. Robin came inside with my toiletry bag and turned on the shower. She knelt beside me and stroked my hair. "You can do this Katie. The shower will help, if only for a little while." I stood up from the toilet and stepped into the shower.

The hot water rushed over me. I turned to face it and closed my eyes. The world outside that shower stall was too much. We had to make decisions. We would ask for an autopsy, but would it give us any answers? Not likely. Would we choose cremation or burial? Should we have a funeral service? How would we tell everyone that she died?

Was I even still a mother?

I'm never getting out of this shower, I thought. I was prepared for so much, but I wasn't prepared for any of this.

I hid in the shower until the skin on my fingers started to wrinkle. Reluctantly, I turned off the hot water and wrapped myself in a towel. Robin came into the bathroom and helped me into a pair of stretchy mesh underwear equipped with the biggest pad I'd ever seen. I was thankful for her help. I trusted her completely. Her heart was breaking too, and she stayed strong for me.

I crawled right back into bed, and Robin placed Poppy back into my arms. Time crept forward. I was desperate to leave the hospital, to run away from our fate, and yet leaving meant saying goodbye to our little girl. No one should ever have to leave their baby behind.

Our friend Suz arrived that evening to help us prepare for life after the hospital. Suz and Eli were best friends; she was his wing woman the night he and I first met. She threw his birthday party when he and I first watched *The Princess Bride* together. Suz was warm, caring, brilliant, and organized. Very few people got to meet Poppy, but she was one of them.

Suz asked if she could organize a Meal Train for us. We hadn't planned on requesting that kind of help, but under the circumstances, we agreed to it. Eli and I had no notion of what life would feel like once we stepped outside the four walls of our hospital room. It would be a challenge to focus on shopping, cooking, and feeding ourselves, but we didn't know that yet. We were still deeply in shock.

We put together a list of groceries for Suz to drop off at our townhouse before we got home the next day. Thinking about food was exhausting. I hadn't eaten anything since we got to the hospital, and my appetite was gone. Eventually, we would both need to eat, and organizing food was practical. Eli and I were grateful for Suz's foresight and kindness.

That evening a volunteer named David, from the non-profit organization Now I Lay Me Down to Sleep, took pictures of me, Eli, and Poppy. Eli and I held her and did our best to look like a family. She wore her white crocheted hat with a tiny pink flower, and the hospital swaddling blanket wrapped loosely around her body. Earlier that afternoon, I'd considered dressing her in a onesie, but it seemed pointless. She wasn't a doll, and I didn't want to pretend.

I'm glad we have those pictures, although they are heartbreaking to look at. I remember the photographer asking us to pose this way and that. To wrap her tiny hand around our finger, to cup her little feet in our hands. To move closer to one another or apart, to lift our chins just a tad, or to look down at her face. David was doing his best, and we were willing participants in the saddest photoshoot of all time.

I'd had enough after about fifteen minutes and asked if we could stop. I needed the day to end.

We thanked David for his service, and Robin escorted him outside. He would send us a copy of the pictures after processing them. A nurse came into our room and asked me if I'd like an Ambien to help me sleep. Without hesitation I said yes. I wished Eli could have a sleeping pill too, but he wasn't a patient. Both of us had had an extremely hard day. He would spend the night with me in the room and sleep on the daybed they provided for partners.

The nurse came back in with the sleeping pill, and I swallowed it with a full glass of water. As I lay down for the final time that day, Eli crawled into bed with me. We shuffled around the sheets and blankets so we could cuddle together for a little while.

"I love you, Katie." He stroked my hair and planted gentle kisses on my cheeks and around my eyes.

"I love you too, Eli." I looked into his brown eyes for any sign of hope.

He read my mind. "I'm not sure how, but I know we are going to get through this."

"Me too, honey." I let out a long sigh. "I'm really tired. I hope you can get some sleep." Tears welled up and streamed down my face. "I'm so sorry. I'm so sorry. I'm so sorry," was all I could say, and then I closed my eyes and drifted off.

Poppy rested silently in the bassinet against the wall. She never left our sight.

CHAPTER 8:

SAYING GOODBYE

———

Light seeped through my eyelids. I regained consciousness from a heavy sleep and sat up in bed. Grief hit me like a tidal wave so great it took my breath away. My baby was in the bassinet against the wall. Still in the exact position from the night before. Her blanket had not moved. She never made a sound. There was nothing anyone could do.

Poppy was dead, and I would have to live with that.

A primal sound worked its way from deep within my gut and out of my throat. It frightened me. It was the sound of desperation. I looked over at Eli, who was lying face down on the daybed. The sheets no longer covered him but dragged on the floor. A pillow over his face to block out the light.

Sadness pressed on my chest threatening to suffocate me. I allowed myself to feel the pressure, then fought back as a violent rage blew through my body. I screamed and collapsed back into tears.

Eli leapt up from the couch and rushed to my side. The door to our room flung open, and Karen, one of our nurses, came inside.

"What can I do, Katie?" Eli asked with concern. Karen stood at a respectful distance and let us talk.

I looked at my frazzled husband and shrugged. "I don't know. Hold me?" I sobbed. He crawled into bed as he'd done the night before, and we spooned.

"Did you sleep?" I asked, wiping away my tears with the corner of the bedsheet.

"Not really. I mean I tried. I mostly tossed and turned. That bed is horrible, and I had a million thoughts running through my head. I think I fell asleep just as the sun was coming up."

"I'm sorry honey. I just want to go home. I really don't want to be here anymore." I looked over at Poppy in the bassinet. Going home meant leaving our baby. I wanted so much that I couldn't have.

Karen interrupted politely to ask if we wanted breakfast. I still wasn't hungry.

"No, thank you. We do want to go home though. Do you know when we can leave?" I asked.

"I'll have the midwife come in to talk with you, okay? I don't think there's much left to do. Some paperwork, and if you'd like to, we encourage you to consult with a social worker before you leave."

"Okay. Can you check on the status of my milk donation application? Also, I need to talk with Nurturing Expressions about getting my breast pump delivered. I should probably express more colostrum, don't you think? Can you get me the supplies for that?" I wiped away more tears. I was trying to take back control over our hopeless situation. I needed to feel purposeful. "I'm sorry for screaming, Karen. I hope I didn't scare anyone."

Karen walked over to the bed and picked up my hand into hers. "Katie, please don't apologize. You haven't done anything wrong. I'll go get those supplies and be right back." Eli and I waited.

Each moment was filled with a vast emptiness. What now? I wanted to hold our baby, so I got out of bed and encouraged Eli to fall asleep if he could.

I walked over to Poppy where she rested. I opened the window shades next to her and let the soft October light stream in on her face. I had never been this close to death. Poppy's skin had changed color, grayer than before. Her lips were deep purple. I touched her cheeks gently with the back of my hand.

Cold.

I loosened the swaddling blanket and looked at her body. Her legs were long like mine, and she had Eli's wrinkly feet. I tried scooping her up to hold her against my chest, but she was stiff. I took a deep breath and thought it through. I fluffed the pillow from Eli's daybed and laid Poppy on it. I sat down on the daybed and placed the pillow with Poppy in my lap. That was the best I could do. I would sit there with her for most of the day.

I recall hearing my father's voice on the phone that morning, but I don't remember much of our conversation. I remember his tears. "How could this have happened, sweetheart?" he asked.

"I don't know Daddy. We may never know. We've decided to get an autopsy, but the midwives warned us there are rarely ever answers." None of this seemed real or made any sense. I was numb and enraged all at once.

The day moved at a glacial pace. The social worker wasn't available until the afternoon, and we understood she had resources and important information to share with us. Around lunchtime I heard the painful screams of a mother in labor coming from the suite behind ours. Then I heard her baby's first cries, and the room erupted in celebration.

Every cell in my body cringed with jealousy. I wanted to be happy for her, but I hated her instead.

Kirsten came to see us that afternoon. She took the afternoon off work so she could drive us home from the hospital, and it was nice to be in the company of another good friend. She was going to be Auntie Kiwi—another dream come to an end. She held Poppy in her lap for a little while as I had done the entire morning. I was rubbing Eli's feet with lotion on the daybed when Karen came in the room to check on us again.

"Need anything?" Karen asked.

"Yes, please. Could you check in with the social worker's timing again?"

"Absolutely." She started to leave the room but stopped herself. "I hope you don't mind me saying this." She looked at me and Eli. "Watching you two interact with one another has been incredibly inspiring. Even now, as you're rubbing his feet. It says so much about you two and your love for one another. You will get through this; I know it." She turned and left the room.

Eli and I looked at one another and smiled. Kirsten nodded her head in agreement. I allowed the depth of Karen's reflection to sink it. *We will get through this*, I repeated to myself. Karen had said so.

I've never forgotten her kindness.

We finally consulted with a social worker named Ellen around 3 p.m. I worked with social workers during my career as an attorney, and I appreciated how informed and straightforward she was. She explained that Poppy's body would be transported to Seattle Children's Hospital for the autopsy that afternoon. She gave us a list of funeral homes and explained we only had three days to select someone to perform the cremation. Eli and I nodded dutifully at Ellen's instructions.

Ellen told us about a monthly support group through Seattle Children's Hospital called Parent Support for parents like us. She encouraged us to give it a try, so we said we would. She provided a reading list of books for coping with stillbirth and various secular and non-secular organizations we could contact for guidance. She handed me a pamphlet called *Trying Again After a Loss.*

The day before I had promised to try again immediately, but at that moment, the idea made me nauseous. She reminded me of the risks of postpartum depression and provided a short list of therapists in our area who took my insurance.

She asked us if we'd taken pictures with Poppy, and we told her we had. She was happy to hear that. "One of the biggest regrets some parents have is not having pictures with their child." Then she gave us a decorated linen memory box. It had frilly white lace around the edges and a white ribbon tied on top. "For any memories of her. A lock of hair, perhaps. Or her little hat."

Again, we nodded. There wasn't anything to say. A rush of grief passed through me, and I disconnected from my body. How could a lifetime of love and possibility fit inside one tiny box?

"Do you have any questions for me?" she asked.

"No, thank you. We appreciate your help," Eli replied for us both. This was not what we'd envisioned for our first day as parents. Our time with Poppy was coming to an end.

We said our goodbyes, and she left the room. The midwife on call came in and told us we were free to leave. She handed me two written prescriptions, one for Celexa, an antidepressant, and one for Ambien, a sleeping pill. I stuffed them into my hospital bag. Everything was arranged for the autopsy, and my application to donate milk was pending. We had the supplies I needed for expressing milk, our bags were packed, and it was time to say goodbye.

Forever.

Kirsten left us alone in the room. Eli and I stood together at Poppy's side one last time, and Eli wrapped his arm around my waist as we gazed at our daughter.

"She's beautiful, Katie," he said. I mustered a smile. He leaned forward and gave her a kiss on her cheek. "Bye-bye, sweet girl. We are going to miss you so much." He stepped back and squeezed my hand. "Want a minute alone?"

"Yes, please," I replied. He grabbed our bags and left the room.

I took a deep breath and let the moment sink in. I could hardly believe these were the last moments with my child. We were meant to spend a lifetime together. I wanted to remember her face forever. I needed her to exist, if only in my heart. I pulled out my phone and snapped a picture—the only one I had the courage to take myself. She looked so peaceful lying there, and her chubby cheeks begged for one final kiss.

"I love you, Poppy. I'm so sorry you had to go. I don't understand. We were going to have so much fun together. I promise I'll never forget you."

I backed away toward the door. I couldn't turn my back on her. In a moment, she would be alone in that room, and we would never see her again. I would be alone inside myself, aching and desperate for something other than reality.

I joined Eli in the entryway. The door closed behind me, and I felt a shudder through my spine. In my arms I held a bouquet of white sympathy flowers sent by my friend Althea; the first bouquet of many. I glanced back at our hospital room for the final time.

My world came crashing down in there.

Now, I would have to learn how to build a new life outside of it.

CHAPTER 9:

MY DREAM

———

"Whether we remain the ash or become the phoenix is up to us."

—DENG MING-DAO

Kirsten drove us home from the hospital in our car. I sat in the front with the white bouquet of flowers in my lap, and Eli sat in the back next to the empty car seat. I couldn't bear to look back there. I watched in dismay as rush hour traffic zoomed by. How was the world still spinning? I needed it to stop.

We said goodbye to Kirsten at the front door, and she promised she'd check in on us the next day. I dropped the flowers on the kitchen counter and walked upstairs into the nursery. I went straight for the bookshelf I'd loaded with pregnancy, parenting, and baby board books. I grabbed my copy of *The Mayo Clinic Guide to a Healthy Pregnancy* and flipped to the index. "Death, fetal," "coping with." I turned to pages 542 and 543. A small section, no more than two hundred words, was devoted to "coping with the loss of a baby." I stared at these words: "In rare situations, a baby dies during the course of late pregnancy. This is called an intrauterine fetal death, and the result is stillbirth."

Tell me Mr. Mayo, how rare is "rare"?

I slammed the book shut and shoved it back onto the shelf. I read that entire guide. Who wants to warn a glowing pregnant mother about the ever-present risk of stillbirth? No one. I get it. What was I supposed to do with the guilt raging through my veins? Could I have done something to prevent this, Poppy? Should I have known you were gone?

The doorbell rang. It was Robin stopping by to make sure we had everything we needed. I remember standing with her at the top of our stairs, both of us assuring one another that I was going to get through this, trying to create hope for my hopeless situation. I needed to be alone with Eli, so she didn't stay long.

I hadn't eaten anything over the last day and a half, and finally I had an appetite. Together, Eli and I rummaged through the refrigerator, which Suz had already filled with food. Reaching into the cheese drawer, I pulled out a chunk of Swiss cheese. It was the fancy kind, and I held it up to show Eli. As if rehearsed, we sounded it out in unison, "*Le gruyère.*" We burst into laughter. I held onto the counter, so I wouldn't fall on the kitchen floor.

I remember looking up at him thinking, *we might actually survive this.*

We gorged. Later, we tried watching a movie but turned off the television after a few minutes. We didn't want to be entertained; honestly, we didn't know what to do with ourselves.

Very few people knew Poppy had died. We needed to share the news. Around 10 p.m. that night, we mustered the strength to announce Poppy's arrival with a post on Facebook. Earlier that day, Robin and Kirsten helped us figure out what to say.

We had no explanation, just straightforward words to express a parent's worst nightmare.

Dear Friends,
We are devastated and heartbroken. Our sweet baby daughter, Poppy Annabelle Muir, was born on October 26, 2015. She weighed 7 pounds, 11.8 ounces and was 20 inches long. However, at an unknown time, only hours before her birth, her heart stopped beating, and she died. We discovered this at our birthing center early Monday morning after Katie was already in labor. Poppy is a beautiful, perfect baby who will always live on in our hearts, and she is watching over us from beyond. Thank you for your love, thoughts, and support at this painful time, and as we grieve the loss of our daughter.
Love, Katie and Eli

I sat on the floor in our bedroom with my cell phone in hand and frowned. "I can't believe we have to do this, Eli." I hit "Share" and turned off my phone.

I fell asleep quickly that night but woke up a few hours later to pitch black darkness. As I came into awareness, I held onto the memory of a powerful dream I'd had. Then I reached for my swollen and aching breasts. I needed to express. I left Eli asleep in bed and walked across the hall into Poppy's nursery.

I sat down in the bright orange glider we had purchased for nursing and gathered my supplies. The room was quiet, the only sound was the ticking of a wall clock. Cupping my breast in one hand, I started to rhythmically press, compress, release, press, compress, release. The ticking clock helped me keep a steady pace. In my other hand, I held a teaspoon to collect the colostrum. I sucked it into a tiny syringe when the teaspoon was full. It was a delicate process, and I didn't want to spill a drop of the liquid gold. As long as my body provided, I would collect whatever I could.

It seems impossible looking back, but I felt happiness with each drop I expressed. I don't know if it was the oxytocin or if it was my belief that Poppy's milk would support life for another baby somewhere. Probably both.

After expressing, I closed my eyes and recalled the vision I'd had in my dream. There was fire, chaos, and destruction. I was wrestling with something, a force. Just before waking, a phoenix rose out of the flames, spread its wings, and hovered in the air. Resting back in the glider, I sensed that the dream was a message from my future.

The phoenix myth tells us that something old must be destroyed and transformed to make room for the new. There was always a sacrifice. The sacrifice would make way for the freedom to create the reality I chose. I wanted nothing more than to rise above our tragedy. Whether I'd emerge stronger and more resilient remained unknown.

I looked over at the side table next to the glider and noticed a blank journal that my mom sent in a care package. She included a Post-it inside with the message, "To keep track of memories with your baby. Xo, Mommy." I grabbed a pen and started writing:

10/28/2015 3:23 a.m.

I'm awake. I forgive myself. I forgive Poppy. Poppy forgives me. Poppy is an angel—loved perfectly during her time on Earth—now she is loving us from Beyond. I woke up from a vision of the phoenix rising—a powerful magical bird. I can heal and rise above this pain and tragedy. I will meditate and breathe into and through this experience. I will allow all the feelings to be a part of me. When awful, destructive thoughts come I will not hold onto them. I will not give them power. I will not give them time or credence. I will ask for help. I will ask for other people to give me some of the strength they can spare. I will take care of myself and honor my beautiful spirit and body. I will not forget the joys of pregnancy, the joys of my marriage, the joys of everyday simplicities like a long walk, a hot shower, a nourishing meal. I will remember. I will reach out to those who have suffered before me and those who will suffer loss after me.

I have read that journal entry a hundred times since Poppy was born. My handwriting was meticulous, each word carrying promise and intention. Looking back on my words, I seemed confident and capable. Intuitive wisdom and grace existed within me already.

My actual healing process was extremely bumpy. Grief would take me places I never wanted to go.

I crawled back in bed with Eli after writing in my journal, but I couldn't sleep. I went downstairs and opened my laptop. I wanted to see what people were saying in response to our announcement on Facebook. Our post had a hundred comments already. I had at least twenty personal messages and a handful of personal emails. I turned on my cell phone, and the text message and voicemail alerts poured in.

For a moment, I felt a little less alone.

I grabbed a box of tissues and a glass of water and read every message. As each person expressed their shock and agony over the news, our reality sunk in further. Poppy did not come home from the hospital. I would never know the color of her eyes. I would never hear her cry. As the sky outside turned from black to gray, I wiped my tears and allowed myself to feel the gravity of it all.

Later that morning, a team member from Nurturing Expressions named Joan delivered a breast pump. My application to donate milk was still pending, but my milk was coming in and I needed the pump to establish a supply. Joan showed me how the breast pump worked. We sat together as the machine awkwardly pumped and sucked, but nothing flowed. That was normal, she explained. I needed to keep pumping every three to four hours until the milk flowed. Who knew if I was even going to have a supply? I had no baby to fuss over, cuddle with, and nurse. A lot worked against me.

After Joan left, I crawled back into bed to rest. I'd been awake since before dawn, and already so much had transpired. Eli tucked me in and encouraged me to stay in bed as long as I wanted. I reminded him that I needed to pump around 2 p.m., and he promised to wake me.

When he woke me up later, I was in a fog but felt motivated to attach myself to the pump. I needed a purpose, and it gave me one. I didn't get much milk, but I pushed my disappointment aside. Every drop mattered.

By late afternoon, I was feeling stir crazy and wanted to go outside. We decided to take a walk in our neighborhood. We bundled up for the weather and started walking south on Fifteenth Avenue. The air felt thick, like I was wading through water up to my thighs. We passed our next-door neighbor's house and an immense wave of shame flooded over me. What if they saw me? What if they could tell I wasn't pregnant anymore? What if someone asked, "Where's the baby?"

I tried breathing through the fear. We didn't really know our neighbors, and no one was paying us any attention. Still the fear felt very real. We made it half a block before I started weeping into Eli's arms. He held me there on the sidewalk.

"I can't do it," I bawled. "I'm so ashamed." I thought back to the day I went into labor. I felt so unsettled that morning. Should I have done something then? Gone to the hospital? Called the midwives? Where did I go wrong? Eli stroked my hair and suggested we go back inside the house. "No, please. I need the fresh air. Let's drive somewhere where we will be alone."

We ended up at Lake Washington and walked along a path beside the water. Autumn was in full display, and maple and oak leaves littered the path. The air was calm as I looped my arm through Eli's and stared down at the path in disbelief. I wanted to walk forever and never go home. When I tried to pick up the pace, Eli reminded me that I'd just given birth, and I needed to take it slowly. I had nothing to show for all my hard work, for my misshapen body, for the pain between my legs.

I tried to focus on the conversation we were having about taking a road trip when something caught my attention. I stopped and interrupted Eli mid-sentence. "Shh." I placed my finger to my lips. Hanging by an invisible spiderweb thread, a leaf levitated at my eye level. Suspended midair, the leaf looked like a rising phoenix. I froze, transfixed by the synchronicity.

Eli didn't understand what was happening. I told him about the vision in my dream. Something bigger was at play, and I was getting signs from somewhere. Was it Poppy? Was it God? I didn't know for sure, but I was willing to listen.

I tucked the leaf into my pocket for safe keeping. On our way home we stopped by a pharmacy to pick up the prescriptions for Ambien and Celexa. As I approached the counter to pay for the medicine, the clerk asked me how I was doing. I thought about it for a moment. "Better than yesterday," I replied. She smiled in response, and I thought, *If you only knew.*

When we got home, I opened my nightstand drawer and dropped both prescriptions inside where they would remain, unopened. Then I carefully removed the phoenix-shaped leaf from my pocket and placed it inside the linen memory box we were given at the hospital. Something was unraveling inside me. Who was I now? It was up to me.

What would I choose?

CHAPTER 10:

FRIENDSHIP AND FLOWERS

———

Love and sympathy started pouring in. Cards arrived in the mail daily; I saved all of them. People I hadn't spoken to in years reached out to express their sorrow. Sometimes I wanted to talk, and people were good at listening. Other times, I didn't have the courage to pick up, so I let the calls go to voicemail. We were flooded with thoughts of healing from family, friends, and acquaintances near and far. We cherished all of it.

For the first few weeks, our refrigerator was packed with food. Fully cooked meals and bags of groceries arrived on our doorstep. Food nourished our bodies and our souls and played an important part in our early recovery. Our friend Melissa brought her massage table over and treated us both to hour long massages. Our witchy friend Nina gave us healing energy work known as Reiki. Our home became filled with fragrant, delicate flowers. During a visit, my friend Rachel suggested I save a flower from each arrangement as a reminder of the support we received. All these years later, I have a mason jar full of those dried flowers on my kitchen windowsill.

My best friend from law school, Althea, sent me three e-books for my Kindle: two guides titled *Healing Your Grieving Heart After Stillbirth, 100 Practical Ideas for Parents and Families* and *Empty Arms: Coping with Miscarriage, Stillbirth, and Infant Death* and a memoir titled *An Exact Replica of a Figment of My Imagination.* I remember the note Althea attached to the virtual gift: "Because you are a reader. There isn't a lot out there, but these books got good reviews. I think you'll like the memoir best. Take it all with a grain of salt though. Don't feel obligated to read any of it. I am so sorry. We love you."

During quiet time alone in the nursery after pumping or writing in my journal, I skimmed the two reference guides, but I could only process a few pages at a time. The advice was practical and important, but it made my skin crawl. I resented that I needed it. On the other hand, Elizabeth McCracken's memoir fed my soul. I devoured it, hungry to know that someone else had been through a loss like mine. McCracken was an author and professor of creative writing living in France when her first child was stillborn at full term. She starts the book with the line, "This is the happiest story in the world with the saddest ending." I knew the feeling. Her experience, her perspective, her real-life pain, captured my heart and my imagination.

Her story inspired me to write mine.

"How can I help you, Katie?" My friend Claudia asked in a message the morning after we got home from the hospital. I told her I wanted to keep a candle burning for Poppy, and within hours organic beeswax votives appeared at our doorstep. She slipped a cucumber in the bag too because I'd mentioned my eyes were swollen from crying.

Claudia and I were casual friends, but we never connected very deeply before Poppy died. In the months after Poppy's death, we spent a lot of time together. Her compassion and ability to sit with me in my grief was both a surprise and a gift. One afternoon while we were sitting on her rooftop philosophizing about life, I asked her how she always knew what to say and how to offer help.

"I learned the hard way, Katie," she replied. "Several years ago, a good friend of mine got very sick and was in the hospital for a long time. I was overwhelmed by my own fears around mortality and anxious that I wouldn't say the right thing, so I hardly said anything at all." Claudia looked over at me and sighed with regret. "I checked in a few times, but looking back, it just wasn't enough. I wasn't the friend that I wanted to be."

I reached over and held Claudia's hand. She smiled at my touch. "About a year later, when my friend was much better and putting her life back together, I apologized that I didn't show up for her enough. I told her that I wished I'd been okay with knowing there isn't a 'right thing to say' and that just being there for her would have mattered the most."

"You should write a book, Claudia," I suggested with a laugh.

"You're funny. In all seriousness, my silence was damaging. I had a subconscious limiting belief that 'I won't say the wrong thing if I don't say anything at all.' Our culture certainly doesn't give us training for this."

"That's true," I agreed.

"Anyway, it's water under the bridge. But I promised myself if another friend was sick or grieving or whatever, I would suck up my fears and reach out more. I would stay in the moment and be with those hard feelings and struggles. That friend was you."

I squeezed her hand tightly. "Wow, thank you. I've been amazed at the people who have shown up for me in ways

I never thought possible. Your friendship is making a big difference in my healing. I love you so much for it."

We opened our home to visitors with the understanding that we could cancel a scheduled visit at any moment for any reason. I needed to be with others, to be hugged, to share tears, and to occasionally have a good laugh. Jennifer and Sam, a couple we befriended hoping to enjoy parenthood together, came over with their five-month-old Madeline the week after Poppy died. I wasn't sure how I'd tolerate being near another baby, but I was willing to try.

It took a lot of strength to spend time with Madeline, especially when she got fussy, and Jennifer nursed her to sleep on our couch. I was seething inside myself, angry that I couldn't soothe and nurse Poppy too. Their visit felt worth the struggle when Jennifer asked if we knew the poppy was the flower of remembrance.

"Really?" I asked, shaking my head no.

"I didn't know that either," Eli replied.

"Yeah, it seems fitting. I wasn't sure if I should mention it, but I figured either you already knew, or you'd find out soon enough. The poppy became a symbol of remembrance for fallen soldiers after the First World War. Every year in November there are ceremonies all over the UK and Canada. People wear handmade poppy flowers and decorate their homes and lawns with poppy flowers. It's beautiful. You'll have to look it up."

"We will. Thank you for letting us know." I reached for Eli's hand. Did Poppy know that when she chose her name? Was it another coincidence or a sign from beyond?

Days after announcing Poppy's death on Facebook, a friend of mine from New York City pointed me to Amelia Kathryn Barnes and her story of infant loss. Amelia's son,

Landon, died in 2014 when he was just a few hours old. With unparalleled grace and bravery, Amelia shared her grief, hope, and healing with a growing community of followers on Instagram. She was a yogi whose heart was broken wide when her baby died. I saw myself in her story, and her vulnerability inspired me to continue sharing with my community on Facebook. She hosted a healing yoga retreat for bereaved mothers called Landon's Legacy, which I would attend in Canada the following summer.

I started seeing an acupuncturist named Anita within a week of getting home. I felt like a shell of my former self and thought acupuncture might help me begin to heal. Before beginning our treatments, Anita and I sat together, and she listened without judgment while I cried for everything I'd lost. Then I'd climb onto her table, and she placed tiny needles on strategic points all over my body that helped me relax and connect with my heart. Her touch reminded me that I was alive. Eyes closed; I'd drift into a peaceful slumber. I showed up feeling broken, and with her needles, Anita started putting me back together.

We were fortunate for all the support. Not everyone who experiences tragedy finds themselves surrounded by a community like ours. Despite our immense gratitude to the people who showed up for us, nothing could take away our pain. No amount of sympathy, kindness, or help was going to bring Poppy back. She was gone, forever.

Halloween fell on the weekend after Poppy was born. Alone in her nursery, I pulled out a pumpkin-shaped hat, crocheted at my request by Eli's stepmother, and let myself imagine Poppy wearing it. She would have looked so cute. I was jostled out of my fantasy when I heard the doorbell ring. Kirsten and her boyfriend, Kris, were there for a visit.

I stuffed the hat back into Poppy's dresser and shut the door behind me. When I opened our front door, Kirsten and Kris were in costume straight from Kirsten's work party. Their celebratory mood made me feel awkward.

Kirsten was one of the few people to meet Poppy. We'd been friends for a long time, first as freshmen in college, then after years of living on opposite sides of the country, we reunited as thirty-somethings in Seattle. We'd been through a lot together. I excused myself after welcoming them inside and hid in the upstairs bathroom for a few minutes. I looked haggard. Postpartum recovery is tough, whether your baby lives or not. I stared at my swollen eyes, ashen skin, and misshapen belly. I didn't recognize myself in the mirror.

I took a deep breath and reminded myself I was safe. These were my friends, and I could fall apart if I needed to. They weren't going to judge. I imagined Poppy wanting me to be happy, so I decided to give fun a try. "Who wants a drink?" I bellowed as I made my way back down the stairs.

"I do!" Eli and our guests answered in unison from the kitchen. I mixed up a batch of Moscow mules and poured everyone a drink. We played Rummikub and Balderdash. My competitive nature kicked in, and I wanted to win. At one point I felt guilty for enjoying myself, but I remembered that Poppy wanted me to be happy, and I was able to move through the sadness. Seeing a smile on Eli's face and hearing his laughter gave me something to be thankful for. Joy was still accessible. Our friends left us that evening with lighter hearts, and we rose above the pain, if only for a little while.

The next day dragged on as we sat around our townhouse trying to find things to do. The nursery haunted us, and baby things were all over the house. In previous years Eli and I created costumes together and spent Halloween night out on the town, but that Halloween there would be no costumes and no dancing.

That night we spontaneously gathered everything we had a receipt for and headed to Target with a carload of baby items to return. Several cases of diapers in more than one size. A diaper bag. Nursing bras. Nipple cream. A case of wipes. Burping cloths. Random presents from the baby shower. When we arrived at 10:30 p.m., the parking lot was practically empty.

Standing in line at customer service with Eli, I wondered what we would say when the clerk asked us why we were returning so many baby items. I held his hand tightly and hoped I'd make it through this humiliating experience alive. We got to the front of the line with our overflowing cart, and I avoided making eye contact with the clerk.

"We have returns to make," Eli said and handed her a stack of receipts.

She looked over the counter at our cart and was respectful when she asked, "What's the reason for the return?"

I looked over at Eli and before he could reply, I interjected, "We didn't plan on returning any of these things, but we don't need them anymore." That was all it took. She nodded and processed the returns. Her grace was a huge relief.

Like zombies with a three-hundred-dollar credit to blow, Eli and I wandered around the store for the next hour. I tried on a couple fuzzy sweaters and stared at my body in the full-length mirrors. I had nothing to show for the extra twenty pounds I wore around my waist. Nearby, two employees chatted quietly with one another while they folded clothes, and I felt self-conscious as I pulled the sweaters back over my head. I had to stop myself from interrupting their conversation.

There's a reason my body is so mushy, I'd tell them. My baby just died. But they didn't even know I was there. I was an invisible zombie. It would have made a great Halloween costume. Instead, it was simply how I felt. I remained silent, alone with my thoughts and my sadness. I didn't buy any clothes that night; nothing fit right. Nothing felt right. Nothing was right. Nothing mattered without my baby in my arms.

CHAPTER 11:

FINDING SUPPORT

———

While we were still in the hospital, Eli decided he would request twelve weeks off from work through the Family Medical Leave Act. I had prearranged for twelve weeks maternity leave and had no plans of returning to work before then. We were newlyweds facing an unimaginable challenge, and protecting our marriage felt vital.

Eli was everything for me in the early days of our grief and having him home was an incredible gift. We were inseparable. He helped me slow down when I pushed myself. He shielded me from things I couldn't handle. He played with my hair and told me I was beautiful. He brought me water, tea, hot chocolate, and lattes. He lit candles, tucked me into bed, held me, and wiped my tears. He encouraged and loved me unconditionally; he shared his fears and made it clear nothing was going to tear us apart.

Donating my breast milk gave us a collective sense of purpose during our first weeks home. We did our best to stay on a pumping schedule, but it felt artificial given there was no baby to feed. Still, our effort came from a place of love and healing. He cleaned the pump equipment and carefully labeled the breast milk before freezing it. He brought me cold cabbage leaves to rest on my breasts when they ached, and he even made me oatmeal lactation cookies in hopes that my supply would increase. They were delicious but didn't really work.

I never produced much milk, but when all was said and done, my donation made a difference. The time I spent pumping was mine to reflect on the love I had for Poppy, and every drop of milk was a symbol of hope for my future as a mother.

Eli and I joined a monthly support group for parents who experienced miscarriage, stillbirth, or infant loss. The group met on the first Thursday of the month, and I was extremely nervous riding in the car to our first meeting. It was November 5, 2015, eleven days after Poppy died. Like most new moms, my life started over the moment she was placed on my chest. Only I wasn't counting how many days old my baby was; I was counting how many days I'd been without her.

A million thoughts ran through my head as we made the drive to Seattle Children's Hospital. Who were we going to meet? How long had they been without their child? What type of loss did they suffer? Neither Eli nor I had been part of a support group before; there were so many unknowns.

I was still wearing maternity pants because none of my regular clothes fit, and I hated feeling the stretchy elastic band around my chubby stomach. I had sacrificed so much for no reward. We parked the car in the hospital parking lot and started walking toward the River Entrance to the building. Grabbing Eli's hand, I stopped. "I don't want to do this, Eli. Do we have to do this?"

He squeezed my hand. "We need to give it a try. If we don't like it, we'll never come back."

The meeting room was packed with grieving parents that night. People sat in a circle and in one corner a large table was covered with pamphlets and books about coping with grief after the death of a baby. We found seats and waited in silence with the others until the meeting began. Bret introduced himself as a trained facilitator, told us a little bit about the baby boy he and his wife lost many years before, and explained how the evening would progress. He invited someone to start sharing and a brave soul began telling her story.

One by one we told our stories of love and loss; each story was unique and heartbreaking. I remember listening to one mom lament the fifth anniversary of her baby boy's death. He was born in November, and the entire month was difficult for her. Every year she took several days off around his birthday and let herself fall apart. One couple lost their twins at twenty-two weeks gestation due to a rare genetic abnormality. Another woman had multiple miscarriages, and her marriage was struggling. One couple was grieving the stillbirth of their last viable embryo. They were infertile and there were no other options.

Eli and I held hands and wiped away tears as we listened. We were being exposed to a whole new world of loss, and there was no turning back. Every pregnancy was significant, regardless of how long it lasted. The dream of life was real, and so was the pain of loss.

Before that meeting, I didn't know that one in four pregnancies ended in miscarriage. I'd never heard of intrauterine growth restriction (IUGR) or procedures like dilation and curettage (D&C). I'd never considered the pain associated with years of infertility treatments, only to have the last embryo die too.

How long is this going to hurt? I thought to myself. *Forever?* My hands started sweating as my opportunity to share approached. Would I say too much? Would I fall apart? Bret looked at me when it was my turn. I wiped my hands on my pants and took a deep breath. Through my tears I talked about how much I loved Poppy and how excited I was to be a mommy. I explained we'd only been married for six months and admitted I was scared this tragedy would tarnish our marriage. I questioned whether I'd have the courage to have more children, and I confessed that I didn't know who I was anymore.

When it was Eli's turn, I listened as he talked about losing his daughter and how he was doing his best to support me in every way he knew how. I valued the opportunity to hear Eli express his feelings, as he was often more reserved than I was.

We left the meeting that night knowing we'd return.

Our support group helped us see we were not alone. When the outside world made no sense, the group became a source of solidarity and understanding. It gave us a place to relate, to confide, and to vent without fear of judgment.

Later that month, we received Poppy's autopsy report. Although the results were inconclusive, the report noted a "small placenta" and something called "mild asymmetric growth retardation of the fetus." I went numb as I listened to the midwife explain that the best medical guess was Poppy's placenta stopped providing her with the nutrition she needed. At what point though? No one could say.

I asked if the results suggested we would experience something similar with future pregnancies. The midwife couldn't say for sure but told me about a blood clotting disorder they wanted me to get tested for. If I tested positive for antiphospholipid antibodies, then it was highly treatable for subsequent pregnancies. I made an appointment for blood work the following day.

My heart sank the next week when those test results came back negative. I didn't *want* to have a blood clotting disorder, but after the inconclusive autopsy results, I'd gotten fixated on finding an answer. The guilt was mounting; if something was wrong with me, I wanted to fix it. Why was Poppy's placenta small? What could I have done differently?

November was full of disturbing obligations. We selected a funeral home for Poppy's cremation thirty miles outside of Seattle in Sumner, a town we never planned on visiting again, and picked up Poppy's ashes the week before Thanksgiving. A woman greeted us warmly in the funeral home lobby when we arrived. We told her who we were, and she returned a few minutes later with a shiny green bag filled with tissue paper. If I hadn't known better, it appeared she was giving us a present.

Inside was a small white box with a tiny pink bow glued on top. The box was labeled "Poppy Annabelle Muir, date of death, October 26, 2015."

The sun may have been shining that day, but all I remember was the dark cloud in my heart. We drove home quietly, the bag resting in my lap. It was nothing like we'd envisioned, but we were finally bringing our daughter home.

CHAPTER 12:

SHE IS REAL

———

My parents were supposed to arrive the night we attended our first support group meeting, but they missed their flight and arrived the next afternoon. The trip was scheduled months in advance to celebrate the arrival of their sixth grandchild. Now, I was drowning in sadness, and there was nothing they could do to rescue me.

Spending time with my parents was both comforting and complicated. I didn't want to take for granted that they'd flown cross country to support us, but I had no energy to pretend. I wanted to melt into my covers and hide. As the youngest of three children, and the last to get married, I wanted to make them proud. Instead, I felt like I'd failed.

Shortly after they arrived and were settled in, I invited my dad up to see Poppy's nursery. I wanted to share our creation with him, even if all our effort was for naught. My heart felt heavy as we walked upstairs to her room which was still decorated and ready to welcome a child.

"Here it is." I held my arms open and spun around to face him. He stood at the threshold, and his body froze. Something overtook him, and he fell to his knees. It caught me off guard.

"This makes it all much more real," he cried into his hands. Bending down to meet him, I wrapped my arms around his broad chest. I pulled him into the tightest hug I could manage and started crying with him. "Daddy, she was real. Poppy *is* real."

We held each other until our tears subsided, then we sat in silence and allowed the moment to sink in. "I can feel her presence, Katie," he said.

"Me too, Daddy. She's a powerful force." My dad and I sat together on the nursery floor, and I told him about the support group meeting we'd gone to the night before. Eventually, my mom came upstairs with Eli, and we answered my parents' questions about our experience in the hospital.

As time moved forward, and I continued to grieve, I reflected on that moment with my dad. I couldn't stop thinking about his words that the nursery made "it all much more real." It took me time to understand that for most people, including my own father, my loss was invisible. Because he never saw her, never met her, never held her, it was as if she never existed. Was it too hard for him to imagine what it would be like to lose a child? Are people incapable of imagining or simply too scared?

For whatever reason, the truth didn't hit home until he saw the nursery.

Poppy kicked, hiccupped, wiggled, lived, and died, all within me. No one knew her like I did, not even Eli. No one would ever truly understand the breadth of my love for her or the depth of my sadness. I appreciated everyone who tried, but I was learning to accept that I couldn't make anyone else feel my aching heart. Being her mommy was an honor and a gift. In time, her sacrifice brought me closer to humanity and to my own true nature.

Later that weekend my dad and I took a walk together in my neighborhood. An idea struck me while he described improvements he made to the wooden gate of his backyard fence. "Daddy, would you build an urn for Poppy's ashes?" I asked. My request wasn't outlandish; my dad could build anything. My most prized possession was a meditation table he had built me after moving to Seattle. I spent countless hours sitting at that table in quiet contemplation as my healing continued to unfold.

"I would be honored." He accepted the heartbreaking challenge on the spot.

"Thank you, Daddy. I know it will be beautiful."

My parents did their best to share the burden of our grief during their short visit. When words had no meaning, their presence was enough. They held me in their loving arms and loved me unconditionally. Nothing was going to change that. Still, I was crushed. Would their carefree, joyful daughter recover? It was too soon to tell.

In the following months, I struggled to communicate with both my mother and my father, as my grief took me to uncomfortable places that were hard to describe. I didn't want to explain my feelings. For a while, we avoided each other completely. "How are you?" was too complicated a question and they stopped asking. I prayed for relief from the rage, the jealousy, and feelings of worthlessness. I learned how to forgive myself when I took my emotions out on Eli or my family.

Every breath was an act of faith, and every day I chose to believe that eventually, I'd make it through.

CHAPTER 13:

OUR ROAD TRIP

___

"The journey of a thousand miles begins with a single step."

—LAO TZU

Once Eli's request for time off was approved, we started planning a road trip. We were anxious to get away from Seattle and explore life together beyond the confines of our townhouse. He and I were snuggling on the couch brainstorming ideas when he showed me a picture of the Grand Canyon on his laptop. A friend had just finished a three-day hike to Phantom Ranch, and the canyon's vibrant colors took my breath away. "That's it! I've always wanted to see the Grand Canyon. Now is our chance."

"I'm in," he replied, and we started making our plans.

11/22/15

Dear Poppy,

I keep repeating this thought in my head: "It's not okay that you died." What bothers me in this moment, a mere four weeks since you were due to arrive, is that I'm getting used to you not being here. That is devastating to me. I really don't have a lot more to say right now. Mommy and Daddy are leaving for our road trip in the morning. I wish you were coming with us; I know your spirit will be there every step of the way.

Love, Mommy

We began our escape the Monday of Thanksgiving week. We were loading up the car that morning when it struck me that we should bring Poppy's ashes along for the adventure. "Eli, what do you think if we bring Poppy's ashes on the road trip?" I asked.

"Absolutely, my love. I hoped we would," he replied. I picked up the green shiny bag we'd gotten from the funeral home only days before and tucked it behind the front passenger seat. I made sure to bring the tiny journal my mother had given me so I could continue capturing my thoughts, feelings, and dreams along the way.

On our way out of town, we made a stop at Nurturing Expressions to return the pump and drop off four weeks of frozen breast milk. The donation, albeit small, was evidence of our teamwork, and it made me proud to know that a premature baby would receive Poppy's milk. Plus, my milk wasn't flowing anymore, and I was ready to move on to the next part of our healing together.

We spent the first two nights with Eli's brother John, our sister-in-law Eloisa, and our darling nephew JD on the southern border of Washington. Eloisa embraced us when we arrived and immediately expressed her sorrow for Poppy. We cried together in the kitchen and held hands as I shared how I was struggling. We were there for several hours, however, before John said anything about our loss. I couldn't understand his silence.

In the privacy of our room, I asked Eli why his brother hadn't spoken up. It was becoming clear to us that people fell into one of two camps when it came to acknowledging Poppy's death. The first camp was eager to express their condolences and addressed our loss directly. The second camp was uncertain how to approach the subject and needed a signal from us that we wanted to talk about her. John fell into the second camp, so Eli and I approached him together and shared that we were okay talking about our loss. John was relieved when we approached him, and he vocalized the devastation he felt for us.

During our visit, I saw on Instagram that Amelia Barnes' "rainbow baby" Lily was born. In the bereaved community, a rainbow baby is the baby born after a loss. Amelia's son Landon had died shortly after being born, and she grew a massive social media following when she shared her grief process and experience with pregnancy after loss. I was one of over one hundred thousand followers holding my breath for the birth of her second child. When I saw her post, I threw back the covers where I was resting in bed and ran downstairs to tell Eli that Lily made it alive. It was the happiest I'd been since Poppy died. If Amelia could have another baby, it meant I could too.

We spent Thanksgiving Day with Eli's father and stepmother in Corvallis, Oregon. They did their best to relate to us as grieving parents, but everything felt awkward. Who was I anymore? What did I have to be thankful for? After dinner, I escaped the casual conversation to be alone. I took a long walk, and then sat in their front yard and listened to the birds, the traffic, and my own breath. I craved stillness. Although very little made sense to me anymore, I trusted my own breath. Breathing in, I knew I was alive. On the exhale, I allowed myself to feel whatever emotion pulsed through me at the time.

We left Corvallis the following morning and headed west to the Oregon Coast. As we drove down Highway 101 and into the mountains, my soul started to relax. I stared out the window of our car and let the wide ocean vistas and dense green forests calm my mind from thoughts of Poppy. We hiked among the redwoods with my cousin Kimberly in Humboldt and drank wine with Eli's friends in Sacramento. We spent several days in Santa Monica and did touristy things like visit the Los Angeles County Museum of Modern Art.

The road was liberating. Eli and I shared endless conversations and long, peaceful silences. It felt good to be away from the townhouse, from the nursery, from all the reminders of what was supposed to be. Every mile we added to the odometer was a promising sign we were moving forward.

In Santa Monica, we took a boat trip out to Malibu. My Aunt Shanna, who lived in Los Angeles, joined us for the warm winter day. I wanted to dive in the water, and she encouraged me to do it. I stood on the edge of the boat in my swimsuit and questioned my sanity.

Do things that feel scary, I told myself. *Poppy wants you to be happy.* The cold salty water baptized my aching soul.

I journaled along the way, trying to create a connection with Poppy's spirit. My brain fired thoughts at breaking speed, and my emotions fluctuated without warning. I was desperate to find some meaning behind her death. If a purpose was going to evolve, it was up to me to create it.

12/1/15

Dear Poppy,

I miss you desperately today. Daddy and I are in Southern California. The sun is shining. You never felt the sun on your skin. It's the loveliest feeling. I've never had to think so much about whether we have a soul and where it goes when we die. I know you are at peace wherever you are.

Womb and tomb are only one letter different. My womb was your tomb. It's such a morbid way to think, but it's okay because you were always safe. When you and I touched for the first time, your skin was still warm; my womb was your sunlight, and I did everything I could to show you my love.

Love, Mommy

Eli and I were on the journey of a lifetime, and our love for each other was guiding the way. From California, we headed for the towering red mountains of Sedona, Arizona, where we hiked into metaphysical vortices during the day and gazed on a million stars at night. If there was healing power in those mountains, I was open to it. We hiked to the top of Cathedral Rock, one of the more famous vortices, and I allowed the energy to lift my spirit. The vibrant blue sky and soft December sun filled me with possibility. Sometimes I felt like I was on the verge of a spiritual breakthrough, and other times I felt ready to collapse in exhaustion from the sadness.

We drove north to the Grand Canyon and arrived in the middle of a glorious sunset. As we drove through the main entrance, the sky welcomed us with a brilliant display of orange, pink, and yellow light. We settled into our cabin and anticipated the wonder of the coming day. We were excited to go hiking and even considered scattering some of Poppy's ashes into the canyon.

During my meditation the following morning, I imagined holding Poppy in my arms. She would have been exactly six weeks old. Tears rolled down my cheeks as I pretended she was there. How much would she weigh? What would she look like?

12/7/2015

Poppy,

We made it to the Grand Canyon! We may scatter some of your ashes while we are here.... Please let me know if that's what you want, my love. Send us a sign.

Love, Mommy

For years I'd dreamed of visiting the Grand Canyon, and under our circumstances, I imagined the canyon as a rite of passage, holding answers to the myriad questions in my heart and mind. During breakfast we planned out a four-mile hike, and afterward we drove to the visitor center where we caught a shuttle to the South Kaibab trailhead. We arrived at the trailhead around 11 a.m., and I remember feeling both excited and somber.

The trail made a steady decline into the canyon, and the views were breathtaking. I was still recovering from labor, and my pelvis started throbbing about a mile into our hike. We took a break at a lookout called "Oh Ahh Point" and soaked in the peaceful majesty. We said "hi" to a young couple resting there too, and I cringed when I heard them chatting about the child they were expecting. Two cowboys on horses tipped their hats as they passed with a pack of mules. The cloudless blue sky gave me plenty of space to think, and Poppy occupied every thought. After resting, we agreed we should turn around.

Back at the trailhead, I stretched as we waited for the shuttle. I took off my vest and hoodie and soaked in the sun. It was fifty-seven degrees, a record high temperature for the canyon in December. Back at the visitor center, we shared a latte and ate our picnic lunch. We decided to watch a movie about the history of the canyon and the national park. The theater was practically empty, and I imagined how hectic it must get during the busy tourist season. I was thankful for the space, the anonymity, and the room we had to breathe.

We popped into the gift store, and after browsing the tchotchkes, we agreed it was time for a hot shower and afternoon nap. We walked back to the parking lot and got into our car. The stereo was playing loudly as we started driving off, and I reached for the volume button at the console. I noticed the time.

"Eli, it's 3:39!" I cried. Eli pulled the car over and put it in park. "It's our sign!" I exclaimed with joy.

Poppy came into this world at exactly 3:39 p.m. Eyes glued to the clock, we watched the entire minute with rapt attention. Time stood still, and we received her message. "You may scatter my ashes into the canyon," we felt her say.

That night we made love for the first time since Poppy was born. I was nervous and thought it might hurt, but it was a tender celebration and amazing connection. The next morning, we explored the Rim Trail, a paved trail that runs twelve miles along the edge of the canyon. As we drove from lookout to lookout, we asked Poppy to guide us toward a spot where we would scatter some of her ashes. Each viewpoint had its own beauty, but Eli and I agreed that Hopi Point was our favorite.

That afternoon we allowed our intuition to guide us as we created a ceremony to honor our daughter. We spread out a blanket on the hard red soil, and together we opened the white box from the funeral home for the first time. Her ashes were inside a plastic bag. My hands shook as I removed the bag from the box and untwisted the tie holding it closed.

I'd never seen human ash before. Our daughter's ashes were beautiful. Pink, cream, gray, and green; they reminded me of beach sand. We lit a stick of Palo Santo to cleanse the air. We sat in silence, and I poured a tiny bit of ash into my hand. I walked toward the edge of the canyon, my hand cupped around the ashes, and I prayed. Standing on the edge, I imagined the canyon was a womb, a nurturing and warm place for Poppy to rest. I tossed her ashes, and a gentle wind carried them away.

Before I could stop myself, I licked the fine dust that remained on my palm. It was a bittersweet communion with my own flesh and blood.

Eli went next. He poured a bit of ash into his hand and spent time with Poppy's spirit at the edge of the canyon. Tears lingered on our cheeks as we cuddled in silence on the blanket. "This is 'Poppy Point,'" Eli declared, and wrapped his arms around me. "Now she gets to watch every sunset."

"How perfect." I nuzzled into his embrace and fell in love with him a little more.

We left the Grand Canyon that night after watching the sunset at "Poppy Point." The temperature dropped rapidly as the sun dipped below the horizon, and I wrapped a blanket around my shoulders to keep warm. Eli set up our tripod to capture the rainbow of colors bouncing off the clouds and canyon walls. Overcome by Poppy's presence, I took the blanket from my shoulders and bundled it in my arms as though I were cradling her. As I had the previous morning, I allowed myself to feel her there, swaddled safely in my arms. Her spirit was boundless and unbroken.

The dream of holding Poppy would fade with time, but in my heart, I hold her still.

PART III:

HEALING

CHAPTER 14:

SHARING MY TRUTH

———

"Too often, we underestimate the power of a touch, a smile, a kind word, a listening ear, an honest compliment, or the smallest act of caring, all of which have the potential to turn a life around."

—LEO BUSCAGLIA

12/11/2015

Dear Poppy,

Daddy and I are getting ready for bed. It just struck me that I didn't cry at all today. That's the first time that's happened since you were born. It doesn't mean I love you any less, but it does mean today was a good day. I love you, cutie pie.

Love, Mommy

Christmas came and went. We hung a little stocking for Poppy over the fireplace and placed a "Baby's First Christmas" ornament on the Christmas tree. My father gave us the beautiful wooden urn he handcrafted, and I poured what remained of Poppy's ashes into it. I surrounded the urn with silk flowers and placed it on a windowsill in our living room. Our maternity and paternity leave were coming to an end, and real life would begin again soon, whatever that meant.

Friends from the Burning Man community gave us two round-trip flight vouchers, so in January we took advantage of another opportunity to visit Hawaii. We stayed in Waikiki with Suz and several other friends. It felt good to escape the darkness of winter in Seattle, but as the saying goes, "Wherever you go, there you are."

Grief traveled with us to paradise.

Eight of us gathered for a quiet day at Lanikai Beach on the east side of Oahu. The sand was silky, soft, and white and reminded me of the Gulf of Mexico beaches I grew up on. The crystal blue water was smooth as glass and lapped gently on the shore. In the distance, giant rock islands jutted from the horizon. I welcomed the change of pace from the busy beaches of Waikiki where we were staying in a high-rise hotel.

After setting up our blankets and chairs, I walked off on my own toward the water. The group was jovial, but I felt lonely and isolated in my grief. Approaching the water, I slowed down to watch some children playing in the sand. The youngest was a toddler, and the two older children were probably four and five years old. They ran back and forth from the ocean to a big hole they were digging in the sand. Each had a bucket, and they were gleefully dumping water into the hole.

I was captivated. "Are they all yours?" I asked a towering man who watched over them.

He smiled and shook his head no. "The little one, he's mine. The other two are his cousins."

"What are they working on?" I asked.

He laughed, "A hot tub! They are great builders." I nodded in agreement and looked out at the water. I felt my throat constricting. A pang of jealousy twisted in my stomach.

"Do you have any builders of your own?" he asked.

My heart skipped a beat. Without thinking my hands went to my belly, and I wrapped my arms around myself remembering the baby once there. I knew this moment was going to come someday, but I didn't know when. I could say "no" and move on, or I could tell the truth.

"I did," I choked out. He looked at me quizzically.

I moved closer so he could hear me better. "I did, but she died. Just eleven weeks ago. My daughter was stillborn."

It took a moment for him to register what I said. Then he understood, and he opened his arms and invited me in for a hug. He was at least six and a half feet tall. I accepted his offer and rested my head on his chest. His skin was warm from the sun, and his embrace was strong. When I stepped back, I could see in his eyes that he wanted to know more.

Sun bearing down, waves lapping softly at the shore, I stood with this stranger and told him my story. It wasn't linear, but it unfolded as a beautiful and tragic tale. We spoke of my sadness, the bond Eli and I were creating, the Grand Canyon, my relationship with my body, and our hopes to have more children.

His name was Kevin. He lived close by. He asked me what kind of things I was doing to cope and if I was in therapy. I told him I didn't think I was ready for therapy, but I was writing a lot. He told me his mother died the previous year, and he wanted to write about her life and their relationship. "Keep writing. Your story matters," he encouraged.

He started to cry when I told him we had Poppy's footprints. He could feel the depth of my sorrow. He allowed himself to imagine what it was like. We hugged again, and he thanked me for being so open. I longed for a swim in the cool water, so we parted ways. I dove in, renewed and grateful that my honesty was well received. I never saw Kevin again, but I'll never forget how he inspired me that day at Lanikai.

Travel was our saving grace after Poppy died. It diverted our attention for a few months, but the distraction couldn't last forever. Eli returned to work in late January when we got back from Oahu. My maternity leave was coming to an end too, but the pressures of returning to my job as a disability attorney felt overwhelming. I wanted to go back to work, but I didn't know how I would handle it.

The first day Eli returned to his job was rough. I hadn't been alone for any extended period since Poppy died, and I didn't know what to do with myself. I wanted to be a part of the world again, but I wasn't sure *how* to be in the world again. Eli and I agreed that my priority was to take care of myself.

When it came, sleep was a refuge from the grief. Some days I spent the entire day in bed, only getting up for the bathroom and rummaging through the refrigerator. On a better day I would wake up to send Eli off to work and find myself crawling back in bed a few hours later for a nap. Nothing could harm me when I was unconscious. There were nights too when sleep refused to come.

1/29/16 12:45 a.m.

Poppy,

Mommy can't sleep. I just seem to lie here for hours and hours. Sometimes my eyes are wide open. Your daddy doesn't want me to worry about it, but the sleeplessness adds to my sadness. Did you know that mothers like me sometimes experience what they call "phantom kicks?" I have them every now and then. Tonight, as I lay in bed, I kept thinking I should have known something was wrong. Could we have saved you? Of course, there's no way I could have known, but I'm struggling with a serious case of "the shoulds."

Love, Mommy

I continued cultivating a relationship with Poppy's spirit through meditation. What is a soul? Do we come into this world with a purpose and a mission? Did Poppy know she was going to die before she was born? I gained clarity sitting at my mediation table; Poppy wasn't a baby anymore. She was the essence of love, and I was learning how to tap into her power. The peace I found during meditation helped anchor me when the tidal waves of grief threatened to take me under.

Yoga also helped me open my heart when I wanted to shut down. I started practicing yoga as a way of life in college because it got me out of my head and into my body. While mourning, yoga anchored me to my spirit and provided nourishment for my soul. A few weeks after Poppy died, my friend Rachel gave me a copy of *Yoga for Grief and Loss* by Karla Helbert. Helbert's baby boy, Theo, died of an aggressive brain tumor when he was nine months old. Her book, which became a healing resource for me, was borne out of her own search for peace and unity and the reminder that "we are, and have always been, united and whole." The ritual of sun salutations energized my depleted body and brought me back to my breath again and again. If I became overwhelmed with racing thoughts, I used mantras to help me dispel those negative voices. Even when my heart felt broken, yoga helped me accept the present moment, and I began to trust that I would emerge stronger and steadier than before.

Eli bought me a Fitbit, and I tried to walk ten thousand steps a day. I wanted to have another child, and I honored my body as a temple for that future life. I took long walks along the water at Alki Beach and through the forests of Seward Park. As my physical body got stronger, I imagined what it would feel like to be pregnant again.

My heart was open to possibility and anything that kept me moving forward. If I saw a rainbow in the sky, I imagined it was a sign from a future child. When a heart shape appeared in the steamed milk of my latte, I pretended it was a love note from Poppy. These were little clues on my path to healing, reminding me that I had something to learn from all the heartache.

When Poppy died, I lost a lifetime worth of hugs, kisses, giggles, cuddles, and smiles. I started to unravel, and it was deeply unsettling. Grief was a frequency that I picked up everywhere—the news, the radio, faces of people on the bus. I couldn't turn away. I was desperate to feel control over the confusion, anger, and fear, but I had to sit with the emotions and feel every single one. I was consumed and lonely inside grief's cocoon.

Eli and I were doing the best we could to nurture and support one another. It was messy, and I'd never been good with messy. I remember once we tried making love, but I couldn't focus, and my sorrow pulled me out of the moment. I apologized and asked if we could cuddle instead. I tried to explain what was going on inside me. He held me closely and listened without judgment.

"It's fine, Katie. Really, I love you. Nothing is going to change that," he whispered into my ear.

My friend Teresa suggested I listen to Brené Brown's TED Talks on vulnerability and shame, and she invited me to join a book club that was reading *Rising Strong: How the Ability to Reset Transforms the Way We Live, Love, Parent and Lead*. Brown's definition of vulnerability as "our most accurate measure of courage" and "the birthplace of innovation, creativity, and change" helped me understand my feelings and reminded me that I was courageous. Poppy's death was changing me, and I wanted to find beauty in her sacrifice, but I was scared I would fail.

Poppy's nursery loomed in our tiny townhouse. We had no reason to go in there anymore, so when we got home from our travels in January, I shut the door and ignored it for another month. We didn't have space to store everything in our garage, so we finally rented a storage unit. I couldn't bear the sound of my own tears while I packed up her things, so I wore my headphones and turned the music up loud. Putting everything into storage bins was a strange form of torture. Eli and I agreed we would store her things for a year and go from there.

2/6/2016

Poppy,

Daddy and I took most of your things to a storage unit today. I knew it was going to be hard, but I feel really down in the dumps now. That's all I have to say. The weight of my sorrow is pulling me down. I'm sorry.

Love, Mommy

Life at home returned to something resembling normal, except for the gaping hole where my arms should have been full. We started going out again and hosted friends for dinner. Part of me embraced the opportunities for happiness, and part of me wanted to stay stuck. I was afraid of forgetting her. I was afraid of losing everything else that was important to me. My marriage, my career, and my sanity. Some days I felt empty and meaningless, and on others I embraced the Divine inspiration that kept me going.

CHAPTER 15:

TIME MUST HEAL

———

"Some days, doing 'the best we can' may still fall short of what we would like to be able to do, but life isn't perfect—on any front—and doing what we can with what we have is the most we should expect of ourselves or anyone else."

—MR. FRED ROGERS

The time had come to return to work. I took an extra month off after my maternity leave ended, but I couldn't avoid it any longer. My job as a Social Security disability attorney came with significant responsibility, and I was extremely nervous because my energy and emotions were unpredictable. My clients needed a sharp advocate, and I didn't know if I could maintain the focus I needed to perform. My boss and I agreed to take it a few weeks at a time to see how I adjusted.

The day arrived to argue my first cases back in court. I arrived at the Social Security Administration office in downtown Seattle a couple hours before my first hearing. I wanted plenty of time to deal with any surprises. I didn't know who knew about Poppy's death, and I had a feeling it would be a hard day. It turned out that lots of people knew about my loss, but not everyone.

"Heeeey Mama!" Jack, a vocational expert, sang in my direction as I walked down a long hallway with my client to the hearing room. My heart sank. I suspected something like that would happen. There was no time to respond, so I gave him a respectful nod and kept walking; I was trying to keep things professional. After my hearing, I invited Jack to talk privately in one of the pre-hearing conference rooms.

"Hi Jack. It's nice to see you." I stood rather than sat. I didn't want to get comfortable. Nothing about this was comfortable. "Did you hear what happened to my baby?" I asked, not wasting a moment.

"No, what?" he replied.

"She died." No point in beating around the bush.

"You're kidding." He looked into my eyes and saw I wasn't. The gravity sunk in. He started crying, and I didn't try to stop him. He apologized for not knowing, and I forgave him. It wasn't his fault no one told him.

Moments like that happened again, with the barista at the coffee shop and the owner of the deli. "Where's the baby?" they asked excitedly when I showed up empty handed, but clearly not pregnant anymore. My truth was humiliating. I wanted to run away and never return, but I had to keep living my life; that meant I became the messenger of her death.

When people said things like "everything happens for a reason" or "God has a plan," I would smile through gritted teeth, nod my head, and silently wonder what that "reason" and "plan" was. Often, it didn't feel safe to explore my thoughts on the issue with that person. Their comment came across as a blanket solution to a problem I could never fix.

My experience of isolation was amplified when people said, "I can't even imagine what you're going through." I understood what they were trying to say, but those particular words put a chasm between us. Was it impossible to imagine what it would be like to lose a child or did my pain make them so uncomfortable they refused to try?

Balancing my desire to move forward with my insatiable need to remember Poppy was a heavy burden. I didn't want to become hardened toward the world, but the crippling sense of loss was mounting. I was learning the very real difference between sympathy and empathy. In *The Power of Vulnerability: Teachings of Authenticity, Connection, and Courage,* Brené Brown illustrates the distinction brilliantly—with empathy you grab a ladder, climb safely into the hole with the griever, and listen. Brown says empathy is a vulnerable choice that requires the listener to connect with the feeling of loss within themselves. With sympathy you see the griever in the hole, holler down that you can see it's bad, then retreat to your own comfort zone.

All that said, many people showered me with empathy. They sat with me as I struggled to keep Poppy's memory alive, and they never changed the subject, even when it got uncomfortable. They forged a connection with me by being there, without trying to avoid or fix my problems. They said simple things like "I'm sorry" and "there are no words." They used Poppy's name aloud and in writing: "I'm so sorry Poppy died," "I wish I could have met Poppy," and "Poppy Annabelle is a beautiful name."

Lucia, my friend from law school, wrote me fifteen tear-stained love notes over the course of several months. October 29, 2015: "There is no good way to start this letter other than I'm sorry. Words can really add no comfort during a hard time like this," she wrote. November 7, 2015: "I hope and pray for you and Eli and Poppy all the time. I love thinking of Poppy as eternally loved and joyful." November 13, 2015: "Often when I'm holding my baby, I look down at her and my heart breaks that you can't do the same with Poppy. I start crying and snotting, a real hot mess."

Lucia made me laugh, writing about the minutia of her day and her toddler "eating like a trucker" and "pooing the loudest poos." In January, I told her how much I was struggling with feeling isolated and not knowing who I was anymore. She wrote, "Your struggle is real, and if you want to reinvent yourself, I'm 110 percent behind you." She reminded me there was no right or wrong way to go through grief. "There's just your way," she wrote. "If you're having a crap day, then have a crap day. If you're having a blessed day, then have a blessed day. Everyone supports you, even Poppy." Her words were a permission slip to move through the world however I could manage. "Girl, you've been through the shitter and back. Don't beat yourself up too. You're perfect."

I needed a permission slip to reinvent myself, especially with my work. My caseload was lighter, but the pressure piled up. I did my best to disguise my pain, but my shields were down, and my own trauma impacted my ability to focus on my clients. Before Poppy was born, I represented just over 1,000 clients at their disability hearings. I was a fierce advocate with stamina and emotional fortitude. Eli joked that my mind was a steel trap. From disease to chronic pain, to severe mental illness and every combination between, I did my best to represent the whole human. Now, rather than stand up for my clients, I was identifying with them—their loss, their pain, and their feelings of being abandoned.

I started thinking about resigning only weeks after I returned.

One of my cases was particularly hard to argue. Latasha (whose name I've changed to protect her privacy) was physically, sexually, and psychologically abused as a child but never talked about it until she was in her late forties. Pandora's box imploded when Latasha received job training for child abuse prevention and treatment, and she was confronted with her own history of trauma. Decades of pent-up emotions and feelings came flooding out. Latasha's depression spiraled out of control, and her anxiety was unbearable. She became unhinged by the post-traumatic stress. She started counseling and tried medications, but she didn't get better. Latasha lost her job and filed a claim for disability benefits. I almost cried on the phone the first time we spoke about her struggles.

I thought to myself, *If I don't deal with this trauma now, I'm going to end up like her.* It was terrifying.

A few weeks later I was in court with Sarah (whose name I've also changed to protect her privacy), another client whose story changed the course of my life. Sarah sat to my left, the judge behind the bench, and the vocational expert across the table. The scene was familiar, and legally, Sarah's case was no more complicated than any other. However, I struggled emotionally to maintain my composure.

Keep it together, Katie, keep it together, I prayed to myself. I squirmed in my chair hoping to keep the tears at bay. I was so tired of crying. Sarah's claim for Social Security disability benefits centered on PTSD, depression, and anxiety. Four years prior to sitting in the hearing room, she was making a decent living supporting herself as a data entry clerk. Then, one fateful night, her twenty-one-year-old son died in a gang shootout. In one night, Sarah's world crashed down; her son was everything to her. She had raised him on her own and taught him right from wrong. His death was tragic and unfair. After the shooting, her job gave her three days off for bereavement, and there was a small funeral where people offered their condolences.

Sarah returned to work that same week, but she was a wreck. She tried her best to focus but had a hard time concentrating. She started sneaking out to her car to cry during her fifteen-minute breaks, and her co-workers tried covering for her when her work started to suffer. During lunch breaks she'd sleep in her car to cope. Then she started having panic attacks and obsessing about what other horrible things might happen.

Sarah started calling in sick. She felt alone and unsupported, and although she had health insurance, she couldn't afford to take time off to see a therapist. She started going to a support group called The Compassionate Friends for parents who'd lost children. She said that it helped sometimes and other times it was triggering. Eventually, she quit her job. She started seeing a therapist because she finally had the time and began taking medication for depression. Sarah filed a claim for Social Security disability benefits two years after her son's death.

After reviewing her file for the first time, I called her to connect. We were talking about the support group she attended and some of the other difficult stories she heard there. Then, in a foreboding tone, she said, "They say time heals, but it doesn't. That's a lie. Time doesn't heal anything."

Her words scared me. Frankly, I needed it to be true; I needed time to heal. If time didn't automatically heal, then

I would take an active role in my process. I would do the deep work to heal.

Back in the hearing room, I took a deep breath and pushed back my tears. We were on the record, and it was time for my opening statement.

"Your Honor," I began, "this case is about the tragic death of my client's son and the anxiety, depression, and PTSD that she subsequently experienced." As I articulated the symptoms of her diagnosis, I started hearing my own story. Inability to focus and concentrate. Tearful. Exhausted. No appetite. Oversleeping. Panic attacks. Irrational fears. Anger and rage. I looked down hoping no one noticed as the tears dropped onto my notes smearing the black ink where they landed.

A voice of truth echoed within me. *I can't keep doing this. I can't advocate for others when I'm a shell of myself. If I don't stop to honor my own process, I'll end up disabled, like Sarah.*

We made it through the hearing. I escorted my client to the hallway and poked my head back into the hearing room. I apologized to the judge for crying. It wasn't professional, and I promised him I'd do better.

He looked at me with sincere eyes. "Ms. Duke, you did a wonderful job. You always do. It's going to take time."

"Yes, I know," I replied more to myself than to him. "Thank you, Your Honor. I appreciate your kindness and your encouragement—really, I do. I just feel like I'm scraping by and for me that isn't enough."

That evening, Eli listened as I shared the story of my performance. Why was it so humiliating to cry during a hearing? It wasn't professional, but that wasn't it. I was struggling with the pressure to show up for other traumatized people. At the time, I just couldn't do it. I felt re-traumatized every time I opened another case file. Each life presented another set of losses, pain, and disappointment. It was time to say goodbye to the job, the salary, and everything I'd worked so hard to accomplish.

I resigned at the beginning of May—eleven weeks after returning. In some ways I felt empowered by my decision and in others I felt like my career was stolen from me, too, just like my child. Would I ever return to the practice of law? I didn't know, and at the time it wasn't important. What I knew for certain was this: I had to honor my grief and allow my healing to unfold. I had to show up for myself like I'd never done before.

CHAPTER 16:

A DOG NAMED WILSON

―――

"Your heart knows the way. Run in that direction."

―RUMI

During our road trip to the Grand Canyon, Eli and I started dreaming about adopting a puppy. We weren't trying to replace our child, but we longed for a way to experience our unexpressed love. In our hearts we were already a family, but without Poppy here, it seemed a dog could complete the picture.

We began looking for a puppy and the search gave us something exciting to focus on. Every evening when he got home from work, Eli showed me the latest cutie he spotted on apps he'd combed through that day. We paid close attention to the dogs in our neighborhood, and we narrowed down our favorite breeds. We both liked terriers.

One Saturday morning, we visited the Seattle Humane Society to see who was up for adoption. We didn't adopt that day, but we did complete our adoption application. After handing in the paperwork, a staff member interviewed us. I choked back tears when she asked us the last question: "What would it mean for you to have a dog in your home?"

I squeezed Eli's hand below the counter where we were standing. "It would make us a family," I replied, smiling through watery eyes. "And that's something we've looked forward to for a while now."

It became a habit of mine to scour the Human Society's website for new dogs every few days. I saw the same adult dogs week after week, but never any puppies. In late March, the Spring Equinox, I spotted a dog named Ranger who seemed like a good fit. I called to ask about him.

The volunteer was forthright. "Ranger has guarding issues. Is that something you're willing to work with?"

"Guarding issues? What does that mean?" I asked.

She explained that Ranger was prone to bite, and he would need a lot of work and training to overcome his aggression.

"Thanks for explaining that. Honestly, that's not at all what my husband and I are looking for. This will be our first dog, and we really want a puppy." I felt guilty, but we did not need more trauma. We needed joy.

"Oh, what kind of puppy?" she asked.

"Ideally, a terrier mix." I replied.

"Really? We put two terrier mixes up for adoption twenty minutes ago!"

I practically jumped out of my skin. "Tell me about them!"

"Sweetie is about five months old, with chocolate brown fur. Wilson is about three months old. He's white with black spots, and he's really scruffy."

Wilson. That was the one.

"Are there pictures?" I asked.

"We will only post pictures tonight after we close. That's if they aren't adopted this afternoon."

Eli got home from an appointment around 4 p.m., and before he could get distracted by anything else, I insisted we head to the shelter. I called my mom as we were driving over the I-90 bridge. Mount Rainier was out in all its glory. "We're going to go adopt our doggie! I just know it, Mom. Wilson is ours. Poppy sent him to us. I can feel it in my bones," I told her.

"That's wonderful, honey. Let us know how it goes!" she replied.

We arrived at the shelter around 4:30 p.m. "We are here to see Wilson and Sweetie," I announced at the front desk.

"Oh really? How'd you find out about those two?" a volunteer named Samantha asked, smiling.

"Me!" The lady I spoke with on the phone raised her hand and waved. "She said they wanted a terrier mix. It seemed like fate!"

"Well, let's pull up your file and take a look." Samantha reviewed our paperwork. "Great, looks like you're all set. Let's go meet those puppies." Eli and I followed Samantha to the kennels. I hadn't felt this giddy in a long time.

"We'll introduce you to Sweetie first. If you don't feel a connection, we won't have you touch her, ok?"

Sweetie was a tiny Chihuahua, cute but nervous. I wrinkled my nose. "No, it's not her."

"Sorry, Sweetie," Eli waved at her as we walked away.

We walked to the next kennel, and Wilson bounded toward the fence. His floppy ears looked too big for his head. He had a goofy grin and licked my hand when I held it up to the chain-link fence.

"Hi, Wilson!" I cheered. "It's nice to meet you, buddy." Samantha asked if we'd like to go into the puppy-only kennel with Wilson for a visit. We nodded. She opened the gate and carried him to the kennel wrapped in a rust-colored towel. She set him down inside and wished us luck.

"Okay, take your time getting acquainted. I'll swing by in a little while to check in. You are the first people to meet him. Enjoy!"

Eli and I sat down in plastic lawn chairs and held our hands out to Wilson. He trotted over and rubbed his body in and out of our legs and outstretched hands. I picked him up, and he cuddled up to me and then licked me on the chin. My heart melted.

We hung out with Wilson for about half an hour, and we agreed he was ours.

Before we left that afternoon, several volunteers came by to congratulate us. We learned Wilson was a stray from Stockton, California. One volunteer asked if we would keep his name.

"Oh yes, Wilson is perfect for him," I replied.

"Like the volleyball in *Castaway*," they suggested.

"Exactly!" We laughed.

We stopped at a local pet store on the way home and bought everything we needed to begin life with a puppy. Wilson pranced around the store making everyone smile with his goofy antics. Everything was new and worth smelling, especially the open bins of treats. I was filled with pride; he was my baby already.

That night we gave Wilson his first bath. My sole regret from our short time with Poppy was not bathing her. As I massaged lavender oatmeal shampoo into Wilson's wiry fur, I imagined being with Poppy again. Wilson gave me a chance to work through my sadness, and as the dirty water rinsed down the drain, it took my regret with it.

Wilson and I cuddled on the couch later that evening while Eli made dinner. I wrapped him in a bath towel and held him like a baby. He seemed right at home. Then he started hiccupping. I couldn't believe it. Poppy wasn't much of a kicker, but her hiccups shook my belly on a regular basis and brought me tremendous joy. Like other cosmic signs, it seemed Poppy was letting me know she approved of our new addition.

Wilson was no substitute for our daughter, but he symbolized a new beginning. From that day forward he was my constant companion. He nuzzled into my side when I meditated in the morning, he stretched out onto my yoga mat, and I learned to step around him during sun salutations. We ran in the woods together, and I taught him how to fetch, shake, and high five.

When Eli surprised me with a romantic weekend away for our one-year wedding anniversary, Wilson came too. He made us laugh at the top of our lungs, gave us purpose, and reminded us that we make an excellent team.

Wilson brought me one step closer to feeling whole again.

When we went to dog parks or on walks in the neighborhood, people zoned in on my scruffy, energetic dog. No one cared what I did for work or if I had any children. No one asked me anything that felt intrusive or awkward. In those moments, my history faded into the background, and life was all about Wilson. For that I loved him unconditionally, just like he loved me.

CHAPTER 17:

GRIEF IS AN OCEAN

———

"I am not a drop in the ocean; I am the
ocean in a drop"

—RUMI

As time passed, I understood more about grief and its
insidious nature. Even as I continued to heal, the pain would
impose itself upon me and demand to be felt. Where Wilson's
presence gave Eli and me something to celebrate, we grieved
differently, and it created conflict in our new marriage. We
argued over the little things and sulked in silence. We didn't
know how to navigate the repercussions of our loss together,
and it didn't feel safe to dream about our future.

It wasn't in Eli's nature to talk about his feelings. I begged
him to share what he was going through, but my desperation
made him retreat more. I needed connection and didn't know
how to ask for it. Lashing out never worked, but I felt so alone
and didn't know how else to act. I remember once yelling at
Eli that Poppy's death was ruining our marriage. He looked

at me lovingly and said, "There's nothing *wrong* with our marriage, Katie. And I'm not going anywhere, but I do think we need help."

We'd heard from more than one person that losing a child led many couples to divorce. Those foreboding words made my anxiety worse and became my greatest fear; I'd end up childless *and* alone. We were committed to finding common ground, but we didn't know how. I asked my doctor for a referral to a marriage counselor, and we hit the jackpot on our first try. Janel, our counselor, was trained in emotionally focused couples therapy (EFT), and suggested we read *Hold Me Tight: Seven Conversations for a Lifetime of Love* by Dr. Sue Johnson. We met with Janel weekly for almost six months the year after Poppy died.

Counseling gave us the tools to understand why we were stuck and what we wanted from one another. We learned how to ask for support with love and compassion. Week after week, we identified how important it was for me to feel connected to Eli, and that I was not a problem to be solved. Janel helped me speak my truth and ask for what I needed, rather than expect Eli to read my mind or force him to guess.

In the same way, Eli needed me to give him space and time to have his own journey. His process did not look like mine. He was doing the best he could, given his life circumstances, and I learned to accept that without judgment. He lost more than his daughter when Poppy died. In some ways, he lost me too. I still wanted to be the girl of his dreams, and it took faith to believe she was still inside me somewhere.

With gentle coaxing, Janel pulled Eli out of his shell. I sat quietly on the couch next to him and waited for him to answer Janel's questions. Sometimes his silence was deafening. I had a million words when he had none. How could he not know how to express his feelings? Why did it seem impossible for him to find the words? Over time I learned to trust that he wasn't hiding himself from me or refusing to share.

His silence wasn't personal.

Eli really didn't know how he felt a lot of the time. He was stuck in his own way and struggling to express himself. Little by little, he started having breakthroughs of his own, and I was able to witness the growth as it happened. Those moments were magical and tender, and I found empathy where resentment once lived. We held hands and looked into each other's eyes and affirmed session after session that we loved each other and believed in our partnership.

In addition to counseling, we consulted with a social worker at Seattle Children's Hospital who worked with bereaved parents. We sat next to one another in her office, and she asked how she could help.

"I feel like I've hit rock bottom with my grief," I replied. I was having a hard time getting out of bed in the morning, and I was putting a lot of pressure on myself to be better.

"May I share something that I've learned over time, doing this work with parents like you?" she asked.

"Of course," I replied. I was desperate for anything that would help.

She encouraged us not to think about grief as having a top or bottom, but to think about it like swimming in water. When we were little and learning how to swim, she explained, we needed to be in the shallow end. As we became better swimmers and could hold our breath longer, we challenged ourselves to touch the bottom. We felt a certain sense of pride when we could go deeper. As we got older and increased our skills, we swam in lakes, rivers, and oceans. Sometimes we could still touch the bottom, and as we matured, we became aware of how deep the water could get. We couldn't touch the bottom. We couldn't even fathom the bottom.

She continued, asking us to envision grief as an ocean. "There is no bottom, the depth is unknown, and exploring down deep can be scary, not to mention dark. As you continue to grieve the loss of your daughter, you will gain tools to handle the depth. It will become less frightening and the emotions overwhelming you now won't be as intense. Waves that once took you under will be easier to manage."

My body relaxed as I absorbed the metaphor. I love swimming, and I love the ocean. I was familiar with the waves of grief, and I was learning how to go with them instead of fighting them. If I allowed the feelings to pass through me, I would be able to manage the grief without feeling swallowed by it. I had helpful tools too, like our support group, yoga, meditation, and writing.

Later that afternoon on a walk with Wilson, Eli and I talked about our conversation with the social worker. Her metaphor made sense to us. We were learning to accept Poppy was gone. We were moving forward and navigating life without her, and with Janel's encouragement in our counseling, we were beginning to dream again. The waves were letting up. Where we once felt trapped in darkness, light seeped through.

We also agreed it was a good time for me to find a counselor of my own. Although our couple's counseling was effective for navigating our marriage, I was having a harder time processing my trauma. I asked Janel for her advice, and she referred me to a therapist named Brenda. I called Brenda and agreed to begin counseling the next week. I had never had individual therapy, and I didn't know what I was looking for.

I had no clear vision for our partnership, only that I wanted to feel better.

The experience brought me to my knees.

Despite Brenda's efforts, I left each of our sessions feeling re-traumatized and unstable. Had I been honest with myself, I would have admitted that Brenda wasn't the right fit and red flags were everywhere. The location of her office was inconvenient, and parking was difficult. By the time I arrived for therapy, I was frazzled from traffic and resentful that it took me forever to find a parking spot. There was a shelf in her office filled with children's toys, and although she worked with children, I resented her for not putting the toys away.

Finally, I realized we weren't aligned in our goals. I wanted to work through the trauma of Poppy's death, but instead, Brenda asked me to share every personal trauma as far back as I could remember. Recalling every little thing that ever set my world on end was deeply triggering. I didn't want to answer her questions, but I didn't stand up for myself either. I just performed.

I felt broken, and I wanted her to fix me.

I woke up the morning after my fourth session feeling suicidal—a thousand pounds of shame smothering my chest. My phone started buzzing with a call from my brother, Aaron. When I explained how raw and exposed I felt, he implored me to stop seeing Brenda and made me promise I would call my doctor, Paris. Thankfully, she fit me in that afternoon. Paris helped me reframe the feelings of shame and provided me with the support I needed to feel stable and safe.

"You are going through a transformation, Katie. If this feels like torture, it is. If you feel like you are losing your mind, you are. And although it might be difficult to hear, this is normal." I appreciated her candidness. "You are not the same woman you were before Poppy died. There is no going back, only forward. If you accept the challenge, you get to reinvent yourself."

I wanted to embrace this opportunity for growth. I wanted Poppy's life to have meaning. Despite the rough start, I was willing to find a new therapist, which I did a few months later. However, a lot of work had to be done. I had to learn that therapy wasn't a fix. It is a process of discovery that can be healing and empowering when the relationship is built on trust and understanding. Challenge accepted, I began reinventing myself, day by day, moment by moment, breath by breath.

CHAPTER 18:

SPACE BETWEEN DREAMS

———

I started writing a blog using the website Medium after leaving my job. My grief wasn't straightforward anymore, and writing helped me process the bigger questions stirring in my soul. Publishing stories through my blog gave me the opportunity to process in the moment, with family, friends, and complete strangers. With no job and no deadlines, my life felt unconventional. I was learning to slow down. The transition was exhilarating and unnerving.

When conversation felt too awkward, my writing bridged a gap to deeper connection and understanding. My family lived throughout the country, and although everyone was doing their best to support me and Eli, there were times when it was just too painful to speak over the phone. Someone might say something I found insensitive or triggering, and while no one was at fault, there were plenty of hurt feelings on both ends of the line.

My dad was very supportive of my writing. "You've got a real gift, Katie," he shared the week after I first started posting on my blog. "I already understand more of your experience."

"That makes me happy, Daddy. That's what I was hoping for. Trying to explain myself over the phone is exhausting, and I get anxious that I'm becoming a burden."

"Honey, you'll never be a burden. I'll always listen."

"I know, Daddy. You're an amazing listener. But grief is such a roller coaster. Sometimes I don't know how to respond when someone asks me how I'm doing. Is that a social platitude or do they really want the truth?"

"I imagine they want to know the truth, Katie."

"Well, that's just it. The truth can be too hard to share. Too exhausting. Some people can handle the truth. Other people, I have to candy coat things. Now that I'm blogging, there will be some people who devour every word and others who never read it at all. That's up to them, and it takes the burden off me to repeat myself."

"I understand that completely," he replied. "Hey, I don't want you to candy coat things, okay? I can handle it."

"Thanks, Daddy. I love you."

"I love you too, Angel Pie. I'm proud of you for having the courage to share what you're going through. I'm sure you're going to help someone out there, too."

My relationship with my dad transformed as I shared more of my process through my writing. We had long, meaningful conversations each time I posted, and I was able to express myself more fully each time. He became my number one fan, and his support meant everything to me.

Later that summer, I was waiting at the gate in SeaTac International Airport when my phone rang. "Daddy" showed up on the caller ID. *He must be calling to wish me a safe flight*, I thought. I was on my way to Landon's Legacy, a weeklong yoga retreat for bereaved mothers in Canada.

"Hi, Daddy!"

"Hi sweetheart, how are you?" he asked.

"I'm good, a little nervous. Just sitting at the gate waiting for my flight to Vancouver. I'm on the way to the grief retreat."

"That's right! I forgot about that. That's going to be a wonderful experience. Hey, I know it's not the best time, but I have something important to share with you."

My heart sank. "Oh, okay. What's up?"

"My prostate cancer returned. My PSA numbers are high, and the medicine I was taking stopped working."

I sat in silence for a moment and tried to absorb the information. His cancer had been in remission for over ten years. Tears started streaming down my face. "Daddy, this is awful. This can't be happening."

"I know, sweetheart. I didn't want to add to your struggles, but you needed to know."

"No, of course. I'm glad you told me, Daddy. It's just a lot to deal with right now." I tried choking back my tears. "I gotta go, Daddy. I'm sorry. I love you." I hung up the phone, wiped my face with the back of my hand and stared out the wall of windows at the airplanes lifting off. My heart pounded. This wasn't fair; I couldn't lose my father too. Not now, not ever. I needed him too much.

I arrived in Winnipeg via Vancouver later that afternoon. Twenty-eight bereaved mothers gathered at the airport, and we caravanned two hours east into the Whiteshell Provincial Park for Landon's Legacy. Amelia Barnes had created the retreat to honor her son Landon and to give other grieving mothers a space to reflect, connect, and heal. The week was humbling, transformative, and affirmed I was not alone.

Each morning we gathered after breakfast for meditation, yoga, and journaling. I sat on my yoga mat and listened as Amelia invited us to close our eyes and connect with our breath. Soft music played in the background, while boxes of tissues were placed strategically around the room. The only rule was to allow yourself to feel and be seen.

Amelia's soft voice flowed over the lyrical music. "Is it possible to hold space for joy and grief at the same time? Do you feel guilty when you notice joy returning to your life? Is there a sense that by feeling joy, you are not honoring your loss?"

Tears gathered in the corners of my closed eyelids as I identified with her questions. I let out a deep breath, then I inhaled the support of the mothers surrounding me. We were all trying to find balance between remembering our babies and moving forward with life. I practiced feeling joy in that moment. My thoughts drifted to Eli and Wilson, then the songbirds singing through the open windows. I felt the warm sun streaming on my face. I was present and open, and anything felt possible.

During the retreat I kept a journal and asked myself questions: What would I gain if I stopped wanting things to be different? How am I relating to my mind—with aggression or kindness and curiosity? Where can I give myself permission to feel my emotions more completely?

I also started reading *Landon's Legacy: The Power of a Brief Life*, a touching memoir that Amelia had just self-published. I underlined and circled numerous passages throughout her book, relating deeply to her exploration of spirituality, meaning making, and self-discovery after Landon died. Less than three weeks home without her son, Amelia wrote, "Right now I can't see the big picture, and maybe I'll never understand it, but what I do know is I gain nothing by trying to control, blame, or dwell on the 'what ifs.' I gain so much more by allowing, accepting, and maybe even one day appreciating the 'what is.'" I had the same wish for myself, to embrace what was happening in the moment and to let myself feel it.

I was there to learn how to love myself again, to let go of anger, and to explore new ways of being. Each of us would heal at a different pace, and we didn't need to carry the weight of the world on our shoulders. We had every right to feel joy again. I returned home from the retreat with a renewed sense of hope for my future. I created a daily ritual of meditations with Poppy; I called in her spirit and sought to know her more, not as a baby who died but as a spirit who had something to teach me. She became my guide. Wilson liked to curl up next to me while I meditated. Sometimes he would get the hiccups, and then I felt for sure that Poppy was there too.

Meditation gave me space to be with my emotions. The time I spent in stillness created a clearing, and whether I felt peace or uncertainty, I was learning not to judge. In his book *True Love: A Practice for Awakening the Heart*, Thich Nhat Hanh wrote, "Understanding is the fruit of meditation. When we practice deep looking directed toward the heart of reality, we receive help, we receive understanding, we receive the wisdom that makes us free. If there is a deep pain within you, meditate." I started to understand.

Every day became an act of faith in accepting life for what it was; accepting that nothing was certain. I kept following my heart and asking big questions: What were my values? How could I use my experience to make a difference in the world? Why did Poppy choose me?

At the suggestion of a few friends, I read *Many Lives, Many Masters*, by Brian L. Weiss, MD, and gained a new awareness of my soul's connection to Poppy. Dr. Weiss was a prominent psychiatrist who transformed from a non-believer in supernatural occurrences to an evangelist of reincarnation and the ability to access past lives through hypnosis. After reading his book, the possibility that Poppy and I knew one another from a past life felt very real to me.

Later that year, Eli and I were on a flight to New York City to visit friends, and there was one baby girl on the entire airplane sitting across the aisle from me. I opened my laptop to vent my jealousy and had an awakening instead:

"How is it possible that a heart can love so deeply a life that is no longer here? A life that never fully got to be here. I sit alone with my thoughts, and then it comes to me. Another answer to prayer. Maybe she was fully here—for her purpose. Maybe she completed her soul's mission. A friend suggested to me recently that maybe all Poppy needed in this lifetime was to be held. I did that perfectly from the womb. Did Poppy know how hard it would be to leave me here, trying to figure all this out? She chose me and Eli. She wanted the love we had to give her. Perhaps she knew we would make it through, resilient and transformed. It's a comforting thought. I'm starting to understand things that seemed impossible before. Poppy knows me—my deepest fears and my greatest joy. Some people believe in angels. I believe in my daughter. My throat tightens as I choke back tears. Here comes the flight attendant. I think I'll get a drink. I am waking up to Divinity, and that calls for celebration."

As I sipped on a ginger ale, I realized *my* mission was to learn more about being human—courageous, vulnerable, and kind—and to share that journey with others. Every time I looked within, I understood a little more. Poppy's life was brief, but her gifts were abundant. She was my guide, and I continued to bloom.

CHAPTER 19:

SEASONS OF LOVE

——

The hardest part of moving forward while also carrying the memory of Poppy was discovering my purpose in the world again.

The week after Landon's Legacy, I took a yoga class at a studio in Seattle. The teacher, Nancy, was a new friend of mine, and I looked forward to sharing my experience of the retreat with her. I set up my yoga mat in the first row and enjoyed the entire session. Nancy led us in a peaceful meditation at the end of class, and while everyone sat on their mats enjoying the moment, I quietly asked her if I could share my story with the other students. I'd taken off my eyeglasses before class started and hadn't put them back on yet. I didn't wait to see if Nancy responded yes or no to my request. Instead, I just started talking.

Turning around on my mat, I thanked the group for sharing their practice with me. I told them I'd just gotten back from a grief retreat, and that I'd lost my daughter at full-term eight months prior. The story poured out of me, and I started crying. I told everyone I was committed to my healing, and yoga was a huge piece of that journey. Then I thanked everyone for listening, and people stood up to leave.

A man came up to me and gave me a hug. A young woman approached me with tears pouring down her face to say that her brother had recently committed suicide and there was so much shame surrounding his death that she never talked about it. Listening to me, she realized how much she needed to talk about the pain she was going through. She told me I was an inspiration.

Nancy and I had a few minutes together as she closed the studio, and I shared how much I'd enjoyed the bereaved mother's retreat. We hugged each other goodbye, and I walked back to my car feeling invigorated. The following day I received an email from Anya, the manager of the studio. She wanted to talk about what happened the day before and offered to help me find "a more appropriate" way to express my grief. I felt like such an idiot. I sent a text to Nancy and apologized, asking if I got her in trouble. She texted back almost immediately. "Not at all. You did nothing wrong," she assured me. She only told Anya what happened on the off chance that anyone from class complained about the experience. Still, I felt like an ass.

In her email Anya invited me to the studio for a complimentary yoga class and then for tea at the coffee shop next door. Alone in my living room I felt like the obnoxious kid in grade school who didn't know when to shut up. *What is wrong with me?* I thought. *Who do I think I am that complete strangers would want to hear about my pain and grief?*

Anya and I met later that week. She wanted to understand what I was going through. I explained that I'd just gotten home from a yoga retreat for grieving mothers, and I hadn't re-calibrated to the regular world where yoga class is a quiet opportunity to stretch and unwind. She asked if I'd tried therapy, and I told her I had but it hadn't gone well. I also shared a little about the monthly support group Eli and I still attended and our weekly counseling with Janel. She handed me a brochure from the Women's Therapy Referral Service and explained how the referral process worked.

Sitting with Anya over a steaming cup of tea, I could see that almost a year after Poppy died, I hadn't addressed certain aspects of my trauma, and although individual therapy felt like a failure the first time around, I agreed to try it again. I hired the referral service to help me find my next therapist. I told Judy, the referral coordinator, about my experience with Brenda. She helped me see where I was vulnerable and explained that establishing trust with a therapist was paramount. Rather than looking for evidence that I was "better," she helped me consider what I wanted to accomplish in therapy. What were my goals? Did I feel heard and accepted by the therapist?

Judy helped me understand that a therapist's methodology was less important than the connection I felt with them. She empowered me to trust my instincts. If I didn't like the location or the artwork on the walls, I didn't have to work with that person. She put me into the position of power, and that helped me see the possibility of healing and growth that therapy offered.

Two months after that yoga class, I sat across from Rebecca for my first of many therapy sessions. Rebecca is an art therapist specializing in life transitions, postpartum issues, and trauma. During our first session, I told Rebecca about the dream I had of the phoenix. I remember sharing that if my destiny was to go through something as life-altering as Poppy's death, I was glad it happened in my mid-thirties. It meant I had time to alchemize my tragedy into something beautiful.

We talked about my struggle with anxiety and panic attacks, and I admitted there were many times, especially late at night, that I couldn't stop reliving painful memories from the hospital. She helped normalize my experience and taught me breathing exercises to calm my nervous system. Rebecca and I worked together for five months. Sometimes Mochi, her ten-pound rescue terrier, would curl up in my lap and cuddle with me while I cried. Rebecca explained the impacts of trauma and helped me restore my sense of self-worth after months of unraveling. I was discovering myself without labels—not as lawyer, not as mother, just as human being.

After explaining the human brain's natural inclination to remember negative events, she loaned me a copy of *Buddha's Brain: The Practical Neuroscience of Happiness, Love, and Wisdom* by Rick Hanson, PhD. In a world that could feel alienating and unfair, I began offering myself more compassion. Understanding the science behind my brain's natural response to trauma allowed me to forgive myself for feeling sad and lonely when I thought I should be better. I was learning that I had the innate power to heal myself and reduce my suffering through mindfulness, meditation, intention setting, and positive visualization.

I shed a lot of tears in Rebecca's office; I also shed guilt, shame, and beliefs that weren't serving me anymore. I learned to trust her and found myself processing difficult events from my childhood that impacted the way I saw myself in the world. Rebecca and I also used art to help me access wisdom and healing beyond words. I used pastels, stickers, feathers, beads, construction paper, glue, paper bags, even googly eyes. Rebecca provided the container and held space with me while I created. It was another form of meditation.

I loved art therapy so much, I found myself using whatever I could find at home to express my feelings—acrylics, chalk, felt, mosaic, glitter, beads, shells, random scraps of fabric, and a hot glue gun. Nothing was off limits, and there was no room for judgment. Using my creativity was one more empowering tool toward healing from my past and envisioning a future I wanted to live.

As summer turned to fall, Eli and I dreamed about getting pregnant again. I started praying for my future child and imagined myself as a happy and confident pregnant woman. Eli and I talked about our fears as we discussed what pregnancy after a loss might look like. This time we were aware of how many things could go wrong, and the hurdle to reaching our dreams felt huge.

People asked us if we were ready to try again, and the question made my heart ache. We hadn't "tried" the first time. Poppy was a surprise. I talked with Rebecca about my worries. Part of me felt ready to connect with a new life, and part of me was still stuck. Was I ready to handle another pregnancy? Rebecca suggested we wait and try after Poppy's first birthday, cautioning me that October would be an emotional month.

Rebecca was right; October was a wild mix of emotions. When I slipped into darkness, I focused on the healing I'd done since Poppy was born and practiced self-kindness. Wilson was my constant companion. He and I spent hours hiking in the woods at Seward Park together and playing along the shores of Lake Washington. He helped me get out of my head and into the present moment.

Eli and I wanted to commemorate Poppy's first birthday, so we decided to host a memorial celebration at our townhouse, inviting everyone who supported us over the previous year. In anticipation of her birthday, we mailed over fifty satchels of poppy seeds to friends and family across the country and attached this note to each satchel:

Poppy Annabelle, born on October 26, 2015, will forever remain in our hearts. Let's celebrate and remember her by growing poppy flowers. Thank you for supporting our path of healing by spreading our daughter's love across the Universe.

It poured rain the day before Poppy's birthday. I didn't mind the weather pretending Mother Nature was crying for me. I took a shower before bed that night, and while I washed my hair the song "Seasons of Love" from the Broadway musical *Rent* popped into my head. I knew every word of that musical when I was in high school but hadn't thought of that song in over a decade. I smiled to myself as I hummed the tune. Our first 525,600 minutes without Poppy was a journey into the depths of what it meant to be human—to hurt, to heal, to celebrate, and to love. Always to love.

The following day was unusually dry and warm. I woke up feeling strong. Poppy's bright spiritual force was with us as we celebrated her first birthday with our guests. We ate good food, drank nice wine, and received lots of hugs. Eli and I reflected on the previous year, acknowledging our grief, our growth, and our love for one another. Our guests watched as we planted a blueberry bush in a large terracotta pot that I'd painted with poppy flowers. Eli and I mixed a handful of Poppy's ashes into the soil and said a prayer for her spirit. We looked forward to homegrown blueberries every summer in Poppy's honor. She would always be a part of us, and we would never stop loving her. We gave everyone at the celebration their own satchel of poppy seeds to scatter.

I went to sleep the evening of her first birthday exhausted but also feeling brave; we had survived the first year without her. She was gone, but I was still breathing.

PART IV:

REINVENTION

CHAPTER 20:

PRAYING FOR A RAINBOW

———

As recommended, we waited until after Poppy's first birthday to conceive again. We had no idea what to expect, as we'd never tried getting pregnant before. The experience was part science, part fun, and part trial and error. There was no telling how long it would take, and I had to trust that the timing would work out. As I charted my temperature upon waking, attempting to identify that brief window of fertility around ovulation, I found myself empathizing with every couple who'd ever tried to get pregnant.

We gave ourselves completely to the experience of conceiving, and while it wasn't always sexy, we accomplished our goal after only three months. One evening in early February of 2017, on a spontaneous hunch, I took a pregnancy test as Eli and I got dressed to go dancing. I stared in ecstatic disbelief as the second blue line appeared on the stick. I called Eli into the bathroom and showed him the positive test. He burst into a grin, and we kissed to celebrate.

After kissing, I looked at myself in the mirror. I'll never forget gazing into my reflection in that moment. My eyes sparkled with a mischievous knowing that this was it. We'd done it. A new life was inside me. The Universe was giving us another chance to be parents, and we wanted it completely.

I harnessed faith and chose to believe that soon I'd be holding a breathing baby in my arms. I started seeing a high-risk doctor named Suzanne Peterson at the Swedish Maternal and Fetal Specialty Center. She was a godsend, validating the emotional journey of pregnancy after a loss and honoring both my joy and my fear. She even started reading my blog. As I'd done with Poppy, I wanted to embrace the magic of pregnancy, but I also had to accept that the second time was different. Ultimately, I would take things one day at a time.

I borrowed a copy of *Pregnancy after a Loss: A Guide to Pregnancy after a Miscarriage, Stillbirth, or Infant Death*, by Carol Cirulli Lanham, from our support group and learned that anxiety surrounding my second pregnancy was not only common, but it was also expected. Reading the book gave me a healthy perspective, as well as permission to be both on edge and optimistic. Lanham, whose son Patrick died late in pregnancy due to an umbilical cord problem, reminded me that I was not alone, and many bereaved mothers went on to have healthy, living children. I found that very encouraging.

I decided to start working again and found a full-time temp job as a contract attorney. Compared to my work arguing disability cases, the job was uncomplicated, requiring limited brain power and zero emotional energy. I needed that. I also appreciated the anonymity—no one there knew about my previous loss.

After five months of powerful healing work with my therapist Rebecca, I felt complete, and she supported my decision to stop therapy. I was at an exciting pivot point in my personal development and started working with a life coach named Adam. He and I had met the previous August at an entrepreneurial conference for unconventional thinkers in Portland, Oregon. The conference opened my eyes to a world of opportunities beyond the practice of law. Adam was a trained lawyer turned life coach, and our connection was magnetic. As trusting partners, we focused on the present and what I wanted to create moving forward. Coaching with Adam was so fulfilling that I considered becoming a coach myself, but before changing careers, I had my second pregnancy to focus on.

Like we had with Poppy, Eli and I wanted to know the gender of our rainbow baby, and we were thrilled when we found out we were having another girl.

As I fell in love with the life growing inside me, my meditation practice saved me from drowning in the waves of anxiety that surfaced. One morning, while sitting in stillness, I felt the urge to pray for my children. I placed one hand on my belly and one hand on my heart. I breathed deeply into the space of my womb and let my prayers flow to the Universe.

I believe Poppy was an old soul. Even though her death devastated me, she had to go. It was an honor to keep her safe, warm, and nourished. I loved her with all my being. That's what she needed, to be adored perfectly, and I did that. It's taken a tremendous amount of energy to heal and recover from her loss, and I simply can't go through that again. As I sit here with this new soul growing inside me, I'm asking for a fresh being. Give her boundless energy. Let her be curious and spunky. I need a child who is determined *to be here. Let nothing get in her way of having a long and vibrant life with me and Eli. Amen.*

I sat in the peaceful stillness and listened. Then, like a bolt of lightning, the word "moxie" pierced the crown of my head and landed in my heart. My body tingled with electricity. *Her name is Moxie,* a voice in my head said. The corners of my mouth turned into a smile. I continued to breathe in a slow, rhythmic way until my meditation timer rang. Ten minutes passed. I opened my eyes with renewed faith; our daughter would make it. I couldn't wait to share my revelation with Eli. That night I told him about my meditation and asked what he thought of the name.

"Moxie," he sounded it out for himself. "I like it. But is that a name?" he asked.

"Of course it is!" I giggled. "Well, it is if we want it to be!"

"Alright, let's think about it." Eli was never one to make decisions quickly.

"Think about it all you want," I leaned in and whispered sweetly in his ear, "because that's her name." I wasn't going to argue with the Universe.

Moments of inspiration and hope intersected with moments of feeling overwhelmed and uncertain. As my body changed and my baby bump became obvious, people at my new job, mostly other women, asked questions like, "Is this your first?" When I was pregnant with Poppy, my reply was an easy "yes!" Now the answer was complicated, and the truth felt like dropping a bomb.

Years later, I can still hear my heartbreaking, and often tearful, reply: "No, actually. I had a baby girl who died. I was in labor when we found out she didn't have a heartbeat anymore. Her name was Poppy."

Was I lying if I chose not to tell someone about Poppy? At the time, I couldn't bear the thought of pretending she didn't exist and wasn't my first. As her mother, I felt obligated to continue her legacy and to share what she was teaching me from beyond the veil. During a coaching session with Adam, he helped me distinguish my fear of forgetting from the need to honor my well-being.

When we looked underneath the fear, I realized I could answer "Is this your first?" any way that felt appropriate. It wasn't a lie to reply, "Yes, this is my first." I would never forget Poppy, but I did have to set healthy boundaries and protect my own heart and energy. My coaching sessions with Adam gave me a safe space to explore how I related to myself and my future child during those challenging situations.

Eli and I did a lot of things differently our second time around. As excited and hopeful as we were, we were also guarded. There was no registry and no baby shower. We didn't buy a single diaper or package of wipes, agreeing those could be purchased after we brought our baby home. We emptied the storage unit where we saved Poppy's things and unceremoniously reassembled the nursery in the spare bedroom. Every action required courage. We didn't realize it at the time, but we were both holding our breath.

I spent a lot of time at the high-risk clinic. Every month we saw Moxie growing steadily on the ultrasound, and my heart filled with joy when I saw her squirm. We plastered the refrigerator with fuzzy black-and-white printouts of a heart-shaped embryo, then a tiny body, next a sweet profile, and eventually a very cramped full-grown baby. Because Poppy's placenta was small and that may have contributed to her death, my doctor prescribed one baby aspirin daily starting in my second trimester to promote the flow of nutrients to Moxie. We bought an inexpensive at-home Doppler monitor as well and listened to her heartbeat on a weekly basis. Anything to promote calm.

I left my temp job that July so I could enjoy some downtime before beginning a twelve-month coaches training program in August. Moxie was due in October, and I'd have a few months of training under my belt before she was born. Coaching was a perfect fit for my skills and talents and integrated everything I cared about into an exciting new profession. I could always return to being a lawyer, but law felt like a step back. I had evolved, and as I moved forward, I envisioned making a different contribution to society. I was facing my fears, living authentically, and believing in myself like never before. I wanted to help others do the same.

Was I nervous about all this change? Yes. Did I let those nerves stop me from living? Not at all. Poppy's brief life inspired me to take risks, and the possibility of mothering Moxie kept me looking forward to the future. In July, Eli and I attended a regional Burning Man event called Critical Northwest. We wore fabulous costumes, enjoyed the company of our friends, and danced until dawn believing the next year we would be taking care of our baby. In late August, I camped with my best friend Althea and her family at Detroit Lake, Oregon, for the total solar eclipse of 2017. We swam in the lake, read books in the sun, and watched the eclipse from a pontoon boat we rented. At 10:18 a.m. the sky was completely black, the lake water started rippling, and I felt a supreme connection to Mother Nature and the life growing inside me.

In the last month of my pregnancy, I went into the clinic twice a week for non-stress tests to see how Moxie responded to stimulation. The test results were all normal, which reassured me. As Moxie's October 15 due date approached, Dr. Peterson and I discussed whether I wanted to be induced or go into labor naturally. The decision wasn't easy to make. I wanted to trust that Moxie would come safely on her own terms, but my anxiety was mounting. After considering my mental health, we agreed to induce labor at thirty-nine weeks.

We set the date for Sunday, October 8, 2017, and I stayed open to the possibility of our dreams coming true.

CHAPTER 21:

MOXIE'S BIRTH STORY

"We delight in the beauty of the butterfly,
but rarely admit the changes it has gone
through to achieve its beauty."

—MAYA ANGELOU

The Sunday we awaited arrived; Moxie's induction was scheduled for 9 p.m. I spent the entire day in training with my coaching school. Moxie kicked me on and off all day, reassuring me that she was strong and ready to go. I rubbed my belly and sent her silent messages through my touch. *We will meet soon, my little one. Soon.*

For the sake of my mental health, we were inducing Moxie one week early, and I felt great about our decision.

I was famished when I got home from training around 6:30 p.m., so I started making dinner. Eli's sister, Zoe, flew out from Nashville to support us and had arrived that afternoon. We'd become close friends over the previous two years, and I was excited to see her. Eli and Zoe chatted in the living room while I sautéed chicken and vegetables. "What is going on here?" I joked playfully. "Shouldn't one of you two be cooking me dinner?"

Our doula, Robin, arrived at our house around 8 p.m. I was thankful she agreed to attend our second birth; we all needed another chance for a happy ending. After taking a hot shower and triple checking my hospital bag, we loaded into our SUV for the hospital. I chuckled nervously as I hoisted myself into the car. I was on pins and needles. This was the most important appointment of my life.

We arrived at the hospital in minutes. I checked in with the front desk of the maternity ward, then sat down with my entourage in the waiting room. We weren't exactly sure what was going to happen after that. Mary, our first nurse that evening, came to get us a few minutes later. She invited me and Eli back to the birthing suite and addressed Zoe and Robin. "We will get Katie and Eli settled into their room, and then you all can come back to visit."

As Eli and I walked down the hall to our labor and delivery room, we explained to Mary that we weren't sure if we would be admitted or if they were starting the induction process and then sending us home. She looked at us quizzically, and in no uncertain terms said, "Oh, you're here to stay. We want to keep an eye on you the entire time."

Eli and I let out a collective sigh of relief. Our dreams were riding on this induction. Mary had been briefed on our previous loss, and I had several copies of my birth plan ready to give the hospital staff who helped us. We had gotten this far, but nothing was certain, and nothing would be until our living, breathing baby was in our arms.

Mary showed us around the birthing suite. I was glad we were in a different hospital, in a different part of town, with a different medical staff. Mary gave me a hospital gown, and I slipped it on in the bathroom. When I stepped back into the room, my heart was beating like I'd just run a seven-minute mile. I could see the anxiety in Eli's eyes too. I sat down on the bed and tried to keep breathing as Mary pulled the Doppler monitor toward me.

"Let's find the baby's heartbeat," she said. Her words echoed inside my brain and time stood still.

Eli came over and sat down next to me. He grabbed my hand, and we took a deep breath. The Doppler monitor slid across the warm jelly on my tummy and contacted Moxie's heartbeat almost immediately. *Whoosh! whoosh! whoosh! whoosh!* Moxie's heartbeat was loud and strong, and exactly where it was supposed to be.

"This experience is already a million times better than our last one," I announced with a smile. I watched as Eli's entire body exhaled. I felt protected—not only by the hospital staff and their fancy machines, but also by a force bigger than everything.

Mary secured two monitors with tight bands around my belly. One monitored Moxie's heartbeat, and the other monitored my contractions. The bands were attached to me for the entire labor and delivery. Mary gently inserted an IV port into my right wrist explaining they wanted the port in place if they needed to administer fluids, Pitocin, or any other medicine. The needle stung a little going in, but I was glad we were prepared.

We then invited Robin and Zoe into the room before meeting Terrence Sweeney, the doctor on call. When Dr. Sweeney arrived, we discussed how the induction would begin, and I handed everyone copies of my birth plan. Writing Moxie's birth plan was an act of faith, and the first two sentences were explicit: This is not our first baby! Our first daughter was stillborn at full term.

I wasn't shy and asked everyone present to ensure that all nurses and support staff were aware of our history. As everyone listened, I felt Poppy's spirit permeate the room. Dr. Sweeney explained they needed to assess if my cervix was thinning or opening. After determining those measurements, they would place a small amount of misoprostol on my cervix to help it open and soften. At some undetermined point when my body was ready, they would likely use Pitocin to induce my contractions. After saying goodbye to the doctor, Mary checked my cervix. It was one centimeter dilated, which meant my body was preparing for labor—a cause for celebration.

Mary placed the misoprostol on my cervix at 10:33 p.m. Eli and I coordinated with Robin and Zoe before they all decided to leave. Robin would be on call when we needed her, and Eli went home with Zoe to sleep. There was no telling how long it would take my cervix to ripen, and we agreed Eli would get better sleep at home. I needed to try sleeping too. I began to have cramps, which I assumed meant the misoprostol was working.

I gave goodbye hugs and kisses to everyone and settled into bed. I closed my eyes and prayed for a peaceful night. I slept for about one hour before Mary woke me up to adjust the monitors. She explained that Moxie was moving around a lot, making it hard to get a consistent read on Moxie's heartbeat. I told Mary about the cramping, which had gotten a little stronger, and asked her if that was normal. She surprised me when she told me the cramps were mild contractions.

"Really?" I asked. "You mean I'm already in labor?"

"You sure are, Katie! Your body was ready." I was thrilled to hear this. The doctor warned us that induced labor could take days and require multiple layers of intervention, yet I was only a few hours into the process, and the contractions were already coming on their own.

Mary kept fiddling with the straps on my belly, and after the fifth or sixth adjustment, I scrapped the idea of sleep and changed into more comfortable clothes. With Mary's help, I settled into a rocking chair and tried to get cozy. I grabbed my phone and earbuds and started a playlist of relaxing music. I held my japa mala, a type of prayer bead, in my left hand. Surrounded by pillows and covered with a blanket, I leaned back and adjusted a silk mask over my eyes. It was the witching hour, 3 a.m., and I was ready to zone in.

My contractions came like waves from the ocean, some bigger than others. The music helped me coordinate my breath with the gentle rocking of the chair, inhaling deeply and exhaling slowly. The silk mask over my eyes created a soft darkness allowing my forehead to relax. I'd never felt more focused in my entire life. I'd created a cocoon of protection, and my unborn child was safe and alive within me.

I would not fail this time. I would know the joy of a warm child on my chest. It had to be true. The japa mala passed through my fingers again and again. I rocked myself back and forth and sank deeper into the abyss of labor. The pain was productive, and I could take it. Night faded into day. Mary came in one last time to adjust the bands around my waist. She was getting off work, and a new nurse would be in to assist me. I remember her final encouraging words.

"Katie," she said, "I want you to remember that you can do this. You can handle this pain. You were built for this. Don't forget you have the strength within you."

This is where my memory becomes foggy, and time is jumbled. Eli joined me at some point that morning and helped me order breakfast. When the food arrived, I pushed it away, nauseated by the sight of it. Robin arrived with an iced coffee from the Starbucks downstairs, and I couldn't tolerate the smell. "Please keep the coffee away from me," I demanded. She chuckled and put it away.

My contractions increased in intensity. My medical team inserted a Foley catheter into my cervix rather than give me more misoprostol. I tried taking a shower, but standing was uncomfortable, so Robin helped me into the tub. The warm water felt nice, but the pain in my cervix was extreme. The new nurse Angie popped her head into the bathroom to check on me.

"How are you feeling?" she asked, looking down at me.

I looked up and grimaced. "This catheter is really uncomfortable."

"You can pull it out if you want to. Just reach down and gently tug it out. It might be stuck." I reached down and tugged at the balloon. It popped out, and I felt immediate relief.

"Oh my god, thank you! I love you!" I sang up to her smiling face.

"You're hilarious. And you're welcome."

I didn't stay in the tub much longer; I was getting more uncomfortable by the minute. My rocking chair Zen seemed like a distant memory, and Robin asked me if I wanted an epidural.

"No, I can manage, but how about some pain medication to save my energy?" I replied.

"That's a good idea, Katie. Let me check with Angie," she said.

We got the green light, and I received a small dose of fentanyl through the IV in my arm. I got back into the rocking chair and worked through contractions for another few hours. The medication helped me relax my body and mind as the pain continuously increased. Robin was with me the entire time, grounding me and giving me confidence. I'm sure Eli was there too, but I don't remember his presence as much as Robin's.

There came a point when the contractions were extremely powerful, and the pain frightened me. I gripped Robin's hand, and I looked into her eyes. "I can't handle much more of this!" I moaned.

"That's great! It means you're getting close," she replied in a cheerful tone that made me want to scream. "I'm going to call the nurse. I think it's time to check your cervix."

"Fuuuuck, this hurts." I was full of fire and losing grip with reality.

Angie arrived a few minutes later and checked my cervix. "Good news Katie! You're ten centimeters!" she announced. "You're fully dilated and ready to push. The doctor is on her way."

It was a huge relief to hear that it was time to push. I couldn't wait to meet my baby.

The attending doctor, whose name I can't remember, arrived as my next contraction was coming. I harnessed my energy to push and bore down at the end of the contraction. She was amazed at my progress and asked me to slow down. I was lying sideways on the bed, gripping Robin's hand and the bed rail when the next contraction came. I gave it everything I had.

"Do you want to touch her head?" I heard someone ask. I let go of Robin's hand and felt the crown of Moxie's head. Everything disappeared. One more contraction. The final push. I felt a rush of movement. I heard Eli's exclamations of joy. Then my baby's first cries.

Moxie Phoenix Muir was here. Warm. Breathing. Alive and on my chest. What a beautiful relief; we'd risen from the ashes. Only minutes old, Moxie scooted to my breast and started nursing. This time our baby would drink the colostrum made just for her. Eli cut the umbilical cord, and I was oblivious as the doctor helped me deliver the placenta. The first time, everything went wrong. This time, everything went right.

We went home the following afternoon, tired, but happy. We buckled Moxie into the same car seat meant for Poppy. Eli drove, and I rode in the back seat next to our newborn. It hadn't rained in days, but as we drove across the Jose Rizal Bridge, a rainbow greeted us from Rainier Valley. Eli parked our SUV alongside Fifteenth Avenue South, and I looked up at our townhouse.

Three poppy flowers waved at us from a flowerpot on our deck. They had bloomed while we were in the hospital. Yet another magical sign that we were being loved from beyond.

CHAPTER 22:

DEATH IS A VEIL

———

"Why struggle to open the door between
us, when the whole wall is an illusion."

—RUMI

When I committed to writing this memoir a few months
after Poppy died, I envisioned it as a way to process my grief,
to heal, and to provide hope and inspiration to anyone who
found themselves in my shoes. I didn't know how long it
would take me to write the story or where it would end.

Moxie's birth in October 2017 was an incredible gift to me
and Eli and marked a new chapter for us as parents. As the
demands of caring for an infant occupied most of my time
and energy, I wrote less and less. Was Moxie's birth the end
of the story, the happy ending that we had prayed for? Not
quite. My intuition knew there was more to learn about love
and loss, and the lessons became clear when my dad died in
February 2019.

I feared the worst when my dad's prostate cancer returned
the year after Poppy died; at that time, the thought of losing

him also was more than I could bear. Three years later during the memorial service where we celebrated his life, I realized my relationship with him was a huge piece of my reinvention. Surrounded by Daddy's loving community and vast network of friends, I could feel he wasn't really gone. As his youngest daughter, I was part of his legacy, and his spirit would live on through me, just like Poppy.

As heartbreaking as my father's death was, I came to terms with it almost immediately. Don't get me wrong; I wanted him alive and enjoying life alongside my mother and his seven grandchildren, but that wasn't the reality. His spirit was mighty, but his body was done.

A few days before Daddy died, I wrote a blog titled "The Gifts of Her Death." It was a goodbye love-letter to my dad, and I published it with his blessing. In the blog, I thanked Poppy for teaching me how to accept *what is* with grace and forgiveness. I admitted I didn't want him to go, but I wasn't afraid to say goodbye either. He was in hospice at the time, and my brother, sister, and I were flying home to see him. I asked him to hang in there for us.

He called me the morning after I posted the blog and told me that he loved every word.

"I'm so glad, Daddy. I do have one regret though."

"What's that?" he asked.

"I'm sorry you won't get to read my memoir. I really wanted to share it with you."

"It's okay, Katie." He paused for a moment. "I have an idea. When it's done, I want you to read it to me. I'll be listening."

He always knew just what to say.

***

For a long time I wondered if Daddy's cancer returned because of the stress of Poppy dying though I have no scientific proof. It was just a hunch. Daddy was first diagnosed with prostate cancer in 2003, when I was twenty-two years old and taking my last semester of finals in college. I was starting law school the next fall, and I needed my dad to be a part of everything.

Finding out my fifty-five-year-old father had cancer was devastating. I was so scared he was going to die.

My professors gave me a couple extra days to turn in my work, and I got all A's, exactly what I needed to graduate *summa cum laude*. I remember the phone call I had with my dad the afternoon I got my grades back. "I did it, Daddy! I can't believe it!" I was so proud of myself.

"I believe it, Angel Pie," he replied. "I believed in you the whole time. You always do whatever you set your heart out to do, and you do it the best."

"Thank you, Daddy. This has been so hard. Your cancer. You have to beat this thing."

"I will, Katie. Don't you worry about me. I'm strong. I'll be just fine." Dad was always resilient. "I want to share something with you though, okay?"

"Sure, what is it?"

"I have a wish for you. I want you to enjoy the process just as much as you enjoy the finished product. You are so capable. You can do anything, but you are so hard on yourself. If I could wish one thing for you, it would be for you to enjoy the journey. Believe and trust that no matter your goal, you will accomplish it."

That phone call was almost twenty years ago. My father was right; I am hard on myself, and I have high expectations. But I've come so far. I remember his words when I become self-critical, and now I offer myself compassion.

When his cancer returned the year after Poppy died, I practiced being open with him about my feelings. I'd just returned from Landon's Legacy and wanted to share some thoughts I was having about the afterlife. I stepped outside onto our tiny patio garden and breathed in the fresh air. I was nervous bringing up the subject of death.

I took a deep breath and tried to relax the tightness in my throat. "Daddy, I want to talk with you about what it's going to be like when you are gone."

"Okay," he replied.

"I've learned a lot about death since Poppy was born. She isn't here physically, but she is here in spirit. I don't know if she exists merely because I imagine her, or if she really does exist. I guess it doesn't really matter. All I know is that the more I invoke her energy, the more I feel it."

"That makes sense, sweetheart."

"This is hard for me to say because it's so hard to think about losing you, but I want you to know you will always be with me after you die. Just like Poppy, you will live in my heart, and I will miss you every day. I will listen to your voice in the wind, and I will see you in the sunsets."

Happy tears flowed gently down my cheeks as I poured my heart out. I could tell he was crying too, and although we were thousands of miles apart, our hearts were linked together.

"Oh honey, that means a lot to me. I'm not going anywhere anytime soon, I promise. But when I do die, I will be with you in spirit. I promise I'll never leave you."

That conversation stuck with me when Daddy's health started to plummet. Confronting death was awkward, but I gained the confidence to have those difficult conversations because of Poppy. Going through her loss helped me gain the words to express my greatest fears and deepest longings. One day my father would be gone, and Poppy helped me see that death is a veil, and my relationship with my father could exist beyond it.

When I visited my parents a few months before my dad died, evidence of his decline was everywhere. Bottles of bleach were placed strategically in the bathrooms along with piles of washcloths to clean up after he had an accident. His body was disintegrating. He barely left his chair in the living room, and he needed help getting into bed. I brought him chocolate truffles as a present, and he accepted them graciously. When the chocolates were still untouched the next day, I asked him if he wanted to try one. He looked at me remorsefully. "I can't, darling. They won't taste good. Nothing tastes good anymore."

It broke my heart to see him suffer. On our last night there, he managed to come to the table for dinner. My mom, my sister Kellee, Moxie, Dad, and I held hands, and he offered up a simple prayer thanking God for our food and our many blessings. I was distracted with feeding Moxie, who was fourteen months old at the time, when Kellee asked Daddy if he was okay. His head was drooping close to the table. His eyes were closed.

"I'm sorry ladies," he apologized, lifting his head. "I just don't have the energy right now." Mom and Kellee escorted him back to his chair to rest. That night, I crawled into bed with him to cuddle. I scooted as close to his body as possible and could feel every vertebra in his back. He fell asleep quickly, and I cried softly as I held him. How had it come to this?

I felt frazzled the next morning as I packed up our things to fly home to Seattle. I ran around the house wondering if it would be the last time I saw my dad alive. I was so spacey that I prepared a smoothie but forgot to put the lid on the blender. I turned on the machine and beet juice shot all over the white kitchen cabinets. Kellee told me not to worry about the epic mess; she'd clean it up. I did my last sweep of the house, got Moxie buckled into the car seat, and went inside to say one more goodbye.

"I love you, Daddy!" I leaned forward to kiss him in his chair. "I'll call you from Atlanta during our layover, okay?"

"Sure thing, my love. Give Moxie another kiss from me."

"Will do!" and I was out the door with my mom to catch our flight. The visit was wonderful, despite Daddy's condition, and Moxie got lots of quality time with him. Their connection was magical. Daddy made Moxie laugh at the top of her lungs, and when they cuddled, she'd invariably fall asleep in his arms.

My dad was an incredible father–encouraging, insightful, and kind. Sure, he made mistakes, but I always felt loved and supported by him. Cancer stole everything from him but his spirit, and I don't ever remember him complaining. As his health declined, I called him every day, sometimes more than once.

We were on a Skype call the last time I saw my father alive. Moxie, Eli, and I squeezed into the tiny frame so Daddy could see all of us. He and my mother were together in his hospice room in Georgia. He was in excellent spirits but was obviously tired. My brother, sister, and I had plane tickets booked to go see him one more time. We needed him to hold on for a few more days, and then we'd all be together again.

But Daddy couldn't hold on. He passed away the day before we flew home. I was parking my car at our babysitter's apartment complex when I got a text from my brother Aaron.

"You should call Mom." I set my phone down and noticed pink buds blooming on some of the cherry blossoms. They were defying the cold February rain. I took a deep breath and shook off the chill in my spine. I knew he was gone. I picked up my phone and dialed my mom.

"Hello." She picked up immediately.

"He's gone?" I asked before she could say anything else.

"Yes, sweetheart. He died a couple hours ago."

My heart sank. "I'm so sorry, Mommy."

"Me too, Katie. I just wish he'd held on so you kids could see him one last time."

"Me too, Mommy. Were you there with him when he died?"

"No, I went home to take a shower. It had been days since I'd changed clothes, but he was surrounded by close friends and cousin Pam."

"I'm glad he wasn't alone. I hate to do this, but I've got to go pick up Moxie at her babysitter's. I love you, Mom. I'll see you tomorrow night. I can't wait to give you a hug."

"Me too, honey. Give Moxie a kiss for me."

I opened the car door and stepped into the rain. I looked up at the gray sky and felt the rain mix with my tears. "I miss you already," I whispered toward the sky and then walked inside to pick up my rainbow. When I got back to the car, I buckled Moxie into her car seat, offered her a snack, and called Eli.

"Daddy died."

Eli took a breath, and we sat in silence on the phone together for a moment. "I'm so sorry, Katie." I heard the tears in his voice, then something shifted, and he exclaimed, "Katie, I see them together!"

"What do you mean, Eli?" I asked.

"I see Poppy and your dad. She was there to meet him when he died. They are together now."

I was surprised by his response and didn't know what to say. I'm not sure what I believe when it comes to families finding each other in the afterlife, but I'll admit it was comforting to imagine Poppy and my father together. I took a moment to let his vision sink in.

"Yes, I can see it too. I like that idea." Then other ancestors came to mind. "Grandmother and Grandfather Duke, Aunt Debbie and Aunt Lynn, and Oma—they were all there to welcome him," I said with a smile.

Years later it makes me teary just thinking about it. It's unprovable, but I love to imagine that Poppy and Daddy are together. They must be so happy.

CHAPTER 23:

CELEBRATING A LEGACY

My dad died fewer than twenty-four hours before his three children flew home to see him. I'll never forget the hug I got from my sister, Kellee, when she and I connected at baggage claim in the Atlanta airport. My brother, Aaron, arrived earlier that afternoon and picked us up in a rental car; then we started the long drive south to Thomasville, Georgia, where we grew up.

I sat in the back with Moxie. The circumstances were unfortunate, but it was good to be with my brother and sister. We lived so far apart from one another that any chance to be together was special. Once we were on the road, we called our mom to let her know we were safe and on the way. She asked us to call Father David, the rector of my mom and dad's church, to discuss plans for a memorial service.

Father David picked up the phone, and Aaron let him know he was on speaker, and we were all together.

"Hi, Katie. Hi, Kellee. I'm so sorry for your loss," Father David said.

"Thank you," we replied simultaneously.

"Father David, my mom said you wanted to talk about whether we should have a memorial service this Sunday. Is that something you can pull together so quickly?" my brother asked. It was already Friday afternoon.

"Absolutely. Your dad and I spent a lot of time together these last few months, and together he and I picked out the hymns and scriptures he wanted to be part of his service. We even discussed and got approval to scatter some of his ashes under the live oak tree in the churchyard."

"Wow, that's amazing," Aaron replied. No one had ever been scattered on the church's property before but leave it to my dad to break the mold.

"All we need is your go-ahead for a service on Sunday afternoon. The church will make all the arrangements after that." We agreed that time was of the essence, and Sunday was perfect for a memorial.

"One more thing before I let y'all go. Your dad is being cremated tomorrow. If you'd like to see him, tonight is your last chance. I can meet you at the funeral home at eight. Do you want to do that?"

"Yes," Kellee and Aaron replied in unison. I stayed silent in the back seat, nervous to admit I was afraid to see him lifeless.

"We should get into town around seven; then we will pick up our mom and meet you there at eight. Thanks so much, Father David. We appreciate everything you're doing to help," Aaron said.

"It's my honor. Jim was a dear friend. See you tonight."

I waited to share my reservations until we got off the phone. "You guys," I half blubbered, "I'm not sure I want to see Daddy." The last lifeless body I'd seen was Poppy's. Aaron assured me there was no pressure, and no one would judge me if I chose not to. I let my mind rest knowing I could decide later.

I was so glad to have baby Moxie along with me for the trip down to Thomasville. Moxie brought joy, levity, and innocence to an otherwise heavy experience. We had all looked forward to seeing our dad, hearing his laugh, and feeling the warmth of his big hands in ours. Moxie's presence helped fill the gap left by my dad's absence.

Halfway through our drive south we made a pit stop for the bathroom, and while my brother was inside the convenience store, Kellee and I hung outside. The sun was beginning to set, and the clouds were turning pink.

Kellee held Moxie in her arms and bent down to pick a dandelion from a crack in the cement. She handed it to Moxie, and Moxie held it while Kellee gently rubbed Moxie's chubby cheek with the back of her hand. My heart melted. Kellee picked another dandelion and blew the petals. Transfixed, Moxie watched as the petals floated into the air.

"What did you wish for?" Kellee asked her sweetly.

There was so much to wish for.

Wishing my dad was still alive, wishing Poppy had never died, wishing that life wasn't so hard. Despite everything, I was so grateful for that moment. My heart healed a little more every time Kellee and Aaron interacted with my daughter. They loved her so much, just like I know they would have loved Poppy.

We pulled up to Hatcher Peoples Funeral Home right at 8 p.m. This time the rental car was full; my mom squished in the back seat with me and Moxie. Ben Hatcher, the director of the funeral home, met us outside the building and walked us to the front door. Father David was waiting inside. The last funeral home I'd walked into was the one where we picked up Poppy's ashes.

"I knew your father," Ben said, as he extended his hand out to each of us. "There was no one quite like Jim Duke. I'm honored to meet you and to take care of him now that he's passed away."

We stood in the foyer of the modest funeral home. A few high-backed chairs were in the waiting area, and a pothos plant wound its way up and down the walls, sconces, and bookshelves. Ben pointed to the front room just to our left and said that our father was inside. We could spend as much time as we wanted with him. I felt my stomach churn. Did I have the courage to go in? If I didn't go see him, would I regret it forever?

My mom, Kellee, and Aaron walked into the room together. Aaron looked back over his shoulder and our eyes met. "Take your time," he whispered. "No pressure."

I stood in the waiting room bouncing Moxie on my hip, and then I heard my sister's cry as she greeted my father. "Daddy, I'm so sorry." Next, I heard a gasp from Aaron.

"Oh, Jim," my mother muttered sweetly. I could hardly take it. I needed to be with my family. This was the last chance for all of us to be together.

I pulled back the heavy curtains and stepped into the room. There he was, tucked in for his final rest. His hands were beneath the covers. Only his head and neck were visible. He looked calm. His cheekbones protruded, his face thin and worn. His eyes were closed. He had a nicely trimmed goatee. At seventy years old, he still had a full head of light brown hair.

I sat Moxie down on a chair in the corner and took my turn saying goodbye. I don't remember saying anything in particular. I kissed Daddy's lips and ran my fingers through his hair. I picked up Moxie and walked her over to my dad. I told her we were saying goodbye to Granddaddy, and he was in heaven now with Poppy. We bent forward together so she could kiss him one last time. She seemed to understand.

Then she started to squirm; it had been a very long day. Father David, who had tucked himself out of the way in the corner, reappeared and asked if we could join in a parting prayer together. We held hands and bowed our heads, and he asked for God's love upon us.

We said goodbye to Father David, and we were on our way. I held my mom's hand on the quiet drive back home. Peace enveloped my family, and I knew everything was going to be all right. The next day we met with Father David at Trinity Anglican Church to discuss specifics of the memorial service. We sat in his office on cozy couches, and together we reminisced about the amazing Jim Duke.

Father David shared conversations he'd had with my dad about his mortality, and I felt assured that Daddy was in a good place. That evening we drank wine and ate cheese and charcuterie at Liam's Restaurant. My mom was nervous about being out in public, concerned that a widow shouldn't be enjoying herself just yet. We assured her she was allowed to do anything she wanted, and as a family, we shared our tears as well as a few good laughs.

The church was decorated beautifully with white flowers when we arrived Sunday afternoon for the memorial. The front row pew was reserved for "The Jim Duke Family." I felt special to be one of the honored guests and also sad. Walking down the aisle of the church, I saw faces from my childhood, people I hadn't seen in almost two decades. The service was more formal than I'd anticipated, full of scripture and prayer, but my dad planned it with Father David before he died, and it was a relief knowing his wishes were being fulfilled.

During the service, a funny memory surfaced of me, my dad, and my brother singing church hymns at the top of our lungs. My dad had a beautiful voice, and although he couldn't read music, he was brilliant at following a tune. Trained to sight read, my brother and I would practice harmonizing as the long church hymns dragged from one verse to the next. Sometimes we hit the notes, sometimes we didn't, and we'd laugh at our attempts. I remember my dad looking down at us sternly, shaking his head as if to say, "Don't do that again," a smile always lurking beneath the attempt at discipline. It was no surprise then that my favorite part of the service was singing the hymn "It is Well with My Soul." I didn't know it at the time, but I learned later that the hymn was written by Horatio Spafford after the death of his four young daughters who died when their ocean liner sank in the Atlantic Ocean. According to an article from the Library of Congress, Spafford wrote "It is Well with My Soul" as he sailed over the spot where his daughters drowned on his way to meet Anna, his wife who survived the accident. As I imagine Spafford felt when he wrote the hymn, singing the words "It is well, it is well, with my soul, with my soul" was both soothing and cathartic.

I honored my father by singing this special hymn as loudly as I could. I put my arm around Aaron's waist, and we held the hymnal together. My mom sang sweetly to my left, and Kellee sang less loudly to my brother's right. I leaned my head upon Aaron's shoulder, and I tried harmonizing with the song. It is well…it is well…with my soul…with my soul. He started giggling. I sang louder. It is well…it is well, with my soul! He laughed harder. I could feel Daddy's presence smiling down on us as we made the best of a very hard day.

After the formal service everyone gathered in the Parish Hall for food, drinks, and speeches given by anyone who felt led to talk. The room was full of people from every corner of Daddy's life, his church, the community theater, colleagues, and customers from the car dealerships where he worked, friends from his college football team, even old high school pals. Everyone in my family spoke at the podium, doing our best to capture my father's essence. I had written my speech the night before on a small notepad I found on my mom's desk. I didn't want to overthink it, so I just went with the flow.

"Daddy was a visionary. At times in my life, he saw possibility when I saw none. He called me forward and encouraged me to be my best self. He thrived on human connection. Whatever he set his mind to, he would accomplish. His humility ran deep. From the stage to the car lot, to the backyard garden, Daddy's spirit shone through. He was generous and kind, funny and warm. He was so handsome.

Everyone here knows the power of a Jim Duke embrace because it carried God's love. When I was born into this world, my father's hands caught me. He held me first and lifted me up to take my first breath. I am deeply honored to be here today celebrating my father's life and legacy with you. As his daughter and his friend, I have so much to be thankful for. May we spread love and kindness like Daddy did; he certainly made the world a better place."

Of all the speeches, my mom did it best. Hers was completely unrehearsed and straight from the heart. I was nervous for her standing in front of a room full of people, but her courage was impenetrable. She didn't cry once. She stood at the podium illuminated with a glow that only love could create. My mom spoke of marriage and commitment and what it takes to make it as a couple in this distracting and overwhelming world. She and my father were high school sweethearts, married in college, and celebrated their fiftieth wedding anniversary the year before he died. I was in awe of her strength and vulnerability, admitting to both the hard times and the good. I thought, *I want to be like her when I grow up*, and then I realized I was like her already.

After all the speeches were made, the crowd moved outside to the live oak tree where some of my daddy's ashes would be scattered. Father David dug a small hole with a shovel, and each of us family members were given a chance to pour a bit of ash into the hole. The experience reminded me of when Eli and I scattered Poppy's ashes into the Grand Canyon. It was sacred and felt like the perfect way to end the celebration. I carried Moxie with me to the hole when it was my turn to pour the ash. As she had many times before, she displayed a sense of knowing well beyond that of a toddler. Moxie was learning to talk, and when I bent down to the hole, she said, "Granddaddy," and pointed to the ash.

"Yes, my love. These are the remains of his body, but his spirit is still alive." She smiled at me sweetly, and I gave her a kiss on the cheek.

Father David covered the hole with dirt, and people dispersed after a closing prayer. The afternoon was coming to an end, and I looked forward to relaxing back at home for a while. I said goodbye to a few childhood friends I hadn't seen in ages, especially my friend Abbey who'd played with Moxie during the reception. She promised to check in on my mom after all the initial attention calmed down. I appreciated everyone who came to celebrate my dad with us. He was so well loved.

It's amazing how death and birth bring people back together.

The first year without him was a crazy mix of ups and downs. There were so many times I wanted to pick up the phone for a quick chat or send him a cute video of Moxie or ask his advice regarding my relationship with Eli. Daddy was a grounding force in my life when my head was in the clouds or when depression had me second guessing everything. His nature was to celebrate the small things—a day without pollen in the air, a garden full of ripe tomatoes and jalapeño peppers, a fish fry after a day at the pond, or a good laugh on the phone with his kids. While I still have the chance, I celebrate the small things too—the hummingbirds that perch on my feeder, my orchids re-blooming, a game of fetch with Wilson, and the everyday joys of being a mother to my rainbow, Moxie.

Daddy was a teacher by nature, and he showed me how to live by example. He didn't get too worked up about much of anything. He was loyal, patient, and forgiving. He was crushed when Poppy died and ecstatic when Moxie was born. He encouraged me to face life's adversities head on, and when all else failed, I had his love to lean on. When he was ready to go, he returned to his Source with open arms. I miss him every day, and just like Poppy, he lives on in my heart and in these words.

EPILOGUE

It's a beautiful summer afternoon in the Pacific Northwest, and I'm sitting in my fenced-in backyard with my laptop and a tall glass of homemade sun tea. After house hunting for over a year, we got the keys to our perfect home on October 26, 2018, Poppy's third birthday. We didn't take that synchronicity for granted.

The year is 2021, and we continue to endure challenges of the global coronavirus pandemic. Wilson is lying in the scorched grass next to me; he loves the sun, maybe even more than I do. No longer a puppy, he still has the spunk and playfulness that brought me so much joy when we first adopted him over five years ago. Moxie, who will soon be four years old, is across the street at our neighbor's house so I can focus on writing.

This morning, Moxie crawled into bed with me and Eli, and before I had time to take off my eye mask, she asked me if I'd had any dreams. I lifted the mask, and based on the color of the sky, I knew it was early.

"I don't think I had any dreams," I whispered into Moxie's right ear. "Cuddle with me, and I'll try to remember."

"Okay, Mommy. Let's spoon," she replied as she scooted her body next to mine. "I'll be the little spoon, and you be the big one."

I wrapped my right arm around her tummy and gave it a little squeeze. "I love you so much," I nuzzled my face into her soft auburn hair.

"I love you too, Mommy, more than anyone."

Eli rolled over and joined us in the cuddle. We heard the *click click click* of Wilson's paws in the hallway, and he propped his sweet face onto the mattress and gave me a kiss on my hand. I savored the moment. Life, with all its ups and downs, feels complete in those intimate moments when we are simply loving each other.

Writing this memoir was a labor of love. Choosing to remember Poppy anchored me to a greater purpose and brought me closer to my essence. My losses have shaped me into a more compassionate and empathetic being and capturing my grief in words was a gift to myself, to Eli, to Moxie, and hopefully, to you.

Given the chance, I probably wouldn't have chosen this path—losing my first-born child and then my father was incredibly hard; but none of us escape life without trials and tribulations. No matter how many times I've felt down, I never give up. I harness the courage to keep believing in my dreams, to face my fears, and to create joy. Each passing breath reminds me that life is about love, connection, and forgiveness. Every morning, we are given a chance to see possibility and to make meaning from whatever life sends our way.

While I am amazed at how far I've come, much has stayed the same. As soon as I get comfortable, I'm up against another opportunity for growth in a world that never stops moving. The more I learn, the more I see we are alike. Everyone has fear and self-doubt, and we all want to be loved. With each passing day, I pray for curiosity and grace. I play, dance, and sing with my whole heart. I give myself time to notice and rest.

Motherhood has been an incredible blessing and more challenging than I ever imagined. I had a lot to learn as Moxie grew from a helpless infant into an assertive preschooler. As I navigate parenting, I continue to lean on practices like journaling, yoga, meditation, and prayer. I model patience, empathy, and self-love, as I seek to raise a kind, helpful, and self-aware human being. Sometimes I fail. As I did when I was grieving, I practice self-compassion and remind myself that I'm doing the best I can.

I started telling Moxie about her big sister Poppy when she was a tiny baby. There were many tender moments with Moxie when I would become lost in thought, imagining what it would be like to have two living children. When Moxie was barely two years old, I was rubbing coconut oil onto her skin after bath time, and we made eye contact that felt like our souls were connecting. She gazed at me and in a mellow tone said, "Sister?" as though she was asking a question.

I was taken back. "Your sister?" I asked while I continued rubbing her legs.

"Yes, Poppy," she replied. "You miss her," she stated sweetly.

"Yes, my love, we all miss Poppy." Moxie held my gaze as a tear streamed down my cheek.

"Need a tissue?" she asked.

"No, it's okay. I'll use my shirt." She'd seen me cry a lot. My thoughts flashed back to when I was a shell inside.

"It's okay, Mommy," Moxie reminded me. "It's okay."

I wiped my cheeks with the sleeve of my shirt and met her gaze once more. "Thank you for loving me like you do, Moxie." She nodded.

"Read me stories?" she asked sleepily.

"Yes, I would love to read you stories."

Our exchange reassured me that all my struggles, all my healing, all my love mattered, and for one little girl, it was making a big difference.

Last year we were sitting on the couch getting ready to read a book when Moxie looked at me and said, "You miss Poppy, don't you?" It catches me off guard every time she brings up her big sister, but I'm learning to trust the wisdom in her intuition.

"Yes, my darling. I do miss her. But I'm *so* happy to be here with you." She sat on her knees and puckered her lips for a kiss. I laid one on her.

Ask her if she wants to see a picture of her big sister, I thought. *No*. I immediately second guessed myself. *She's too young. She won't understand*. I picked up the book and started reading, but the thought wouldn't leave me alone.

Ask her, Katie. It's okay. Let Moxie decide. I placed the book in my lap and turned to face her.

"Moxie, would you like to see a picture of your big sister Poppy?"

"I would *love* that," she said resolutely.

My laptop was on the kitchen island and after opening it, I searched for the folder of pictures that inevitably makes me cry. I clicked on the folder labeled "Photoshoot with Poppy" and scrolled through the handful of black-and-white pictures we have with her.

"Here you go, sweetie," I said, setting the laptop on the couch. "This is Poppy, your big sister."

She looked at Poppy's image. "Her eyes aren't open, Mommy."

"No," I shook my head. "They never opened."

She looked back at the picture. "Could she talk?"

"No, sweetheart, she never made a sound." My hands went to my heart. "She grew inside of me for nine months, and then just when she was ready to be born, she died."

"Oh." She thought for a moment and then looked at me quizzically. "But Mommy, she's not a flower."

"No angel, her *name* is Poppy, like the flower. But she was a real baby. Here, let me show you another one." I clicked to the next image, which was of me and Eli resting our hands on Poppy's body.

"Are those my daddy's hands?" Moxie asked.

"Yes, those are his hands, and that's my hand there." I pointed at the picture to help her distinguish.

She took a deep breath and looked up at me. "Oh Mommy, I *love* this picture."

My heart exploded with joy and tears poured out as they had a million times before.

"Mommy, will you read me my story now?"

"Yes, my love. Thank you for letting me show you her pictures."

We cuddled together on the couch and imagined Moxie's future together as I read *The Wonderful Things You Will Be* by Emily Winfield Martin. What a lucky human I am to have these magical children—one in my arms and one in the sky.

Just last week, Moxie and I popped out to the library to grab a new assortment of books for bedtime reading. We opened the front door to our house, and Moxie commented on the California poppy flowers blooming at the base of a large pine tree in our front yard.

"Mommy, look! More poppy flowers are opening!" she exclaimed.

"I know; aren't they beautiful?" I walked around the corner of the house to prepare my bicycle for the ride to the library. I was reaching over Moxie's bicycle trailer for my helmet when she walked around the corner and asked me a question.

"Was Poppy your perfect little daughter?"

I knelt to her eye level and set my helmet on the ground. "*You're* my perfect little daughter," I emphasized as I pulled her into my arms and gave her a big hug.

She pulled back and looked at me with piercing hazel eyes. "But Poppy was perfect too, wasn't she?"

"Yes, my love. She was perfect."

"And you loved her?"

"Very much." I am awestruck by Moxie's ability to hold space with me.

"Why did she die, Mommy?" Her curiosity is so innocent and pure.

"Well, we don't really know." I sat down on the ground. "Poppy's heart stopped beating inside her chest and when that happened, she died."

"But I'm alive! My heart hasn't stopped beating!" Her voice rang out for all to hear.

"That's right. You are alive!" I giggled.

"Granddaddy died, didn't he?" She looked at me sadly.

"Yes, sweetheart. He died too. I miss him every day."

"Someday Wilson will die, won't he?"

"Yes, my little one." I've been teaching Moxie to treat Wilson with kindness, reminding her that he is a living being who deserves respect. "Wilson will die someday. Every living thing dies at some point."

"Can we go to the library now?" She changed the subject instantly.

"Absolutely!" I was happy to get going. It was a lovely evening, overcast but not cold. I peddled up our street feeling free. Moxie sang happily behind me in her bicycle trailer, and the summer breeze refreshed me as it passed through my sweater.

Life was good. Our loved ones were with us, in memory and in spirit, and I was grateful for another day to grow and be present to this beautiful and mysterious thing we call life.

PHHOTOGRAPHS

One of our "first look" moments in Parson's Garden, April 2015.
Image courtesy of Jeff Shipley.

My Dad and me after my wedding—I always looked up to him.
Image courtesy of Jeff Shipley.

A family portrait with our precious Poppy Annabelle on her
birthday, October 26, 2015. Image courtesy of Now I Lay Me
Down to Sleep.

Holding my daughter's spirit at the edge of "Poppy Point" in the
Grand Canyon, December 2015. Photo taken by Eli.

Wilson, our scruffy puppy, the night we brought him home from the Humane Society in March 2016. He was right at home.

The first of many family portraits with Moxie, the morning after she was born, October 2017. Image courtesy of Bella Baby Photography.

The Jim Duke Family at my father's March 2019 memorial service (from left to right): me (holding an urn with my dad's ashes), Aaron, Kellee, Moxie, and Louise.

Moxie and her big brother, Wilson, September 2019.

Celebrating Eli's birthday, November 2021.

OUR LOVE STORY IS MY FAVORITE OF ALL TIME

I first published this open love letter to Eli on January 26, 2017, via my blog. Two weeks later we learned I was pregnant with our rainbow baby, Moxie. That was five years ago, and our love story is still my favorite.

Thank you for choosing me every single day, Eli. Your faith in me and my ability to tell our love story is unwavering. I love you so much.

***

You asked me to marry you on a Sunday. The sun's rays bounced off the rolling waves of the Pacific Ocean, the sky awash in pastel yellow, blue, and pink. The very next day we found out I was pregnant. You were excited before me. I sat in the bathroom and stared at the plus sign on the pregnancy test. You watched through the open door and smiled. You weren't concerned. "But," I bemoaned, "we just got engaged." You beamed. "Good thing I asked you to marry me yesterday!"

We were married ten weeks later during an outdoor wedding in the spring. The sun shone that day and the temperature hit fifty-five degrees, not too cold to wear my sleeveless empire wedding dress. As we shared our vows, I got chill bumps when I promised to be "the mother of your children and the companion of your days."

I was fourteen weeks pregnant. We knew Poppy was a girl, and she already had her name. She'd chosen it just days after we knew she existed. "Poppyseed," we started calling our tiny zygote, the same week we discovered I was pregnant. You loved the nickname.

I remember sitting at the kitchen counter with your laptop when we opened the email revealing her gender. We didn't want to wait. We couldn't wait. We were so excited. We were having a girl. The first girl grandbaby on your side of the family.

You were a prince during our pregnancy. I say "our" because I never felt alone. The weird symptoms and fatigue—we bore those together. You massaged my feet, you made me tea, you drew the bath, you told me I was beautiful, and I felt beautiful.

We took those silly weekly pictures in front of the living room wall. I wore the same outfit. A tie-dyed tube top and pink booty shorts. I flexed my muscles and made you take pictures of my butt so I could see if I was getting too fat. You made me feel sexy. I was sexy.

You kissed my belly every day and touched me tenderly. You went to every prenatal appointment, and you held my hand at our thirty-four-week ultrasound when the midwife was concerned about my fundal height. But Poppy was just fine. All her measurements checked out, and her sweet face cozied up to the umbilical cord. She had hair already.

You panicked the night I went into labor, and as you paced back and forth in the kitchen, I had to tell you to calm down; it made me laugh.

I'll never forget the look on your face when you understood what the midwife was telling us when they couldn't find a heartbeat: Poppy was dead. Your face fell into your hands and your body collapsed. I could feel the life being sucked out of you, and then it was sucked out of me, just like it had been sucked out of our baby girl.

You were a warrior those next thirty-six hours we were in the hospital. Our world was crashing down, and still we were falling in love. You stroked my hair gently and whispered reassuring encouragement as the midwife told me I could push. You didn't look away from my face. I remember that. You were focused on me. Our baby was about to be born, still. You were strong.

How can we ever explain to another human the simultaneous horror and joy of bringing a dead child into the world? That's what we did. All our hard work, our love, our efforts, our expectations, ruined and yet fulfilled. Poppy was here. We'd done it. We had a child together, and she was perfect.

And gone.

You held her so sweetly. You took off your shirt so you could feel her skin to skin. She was beautiful. Everyone who met her would agree. Her eyes never opened. We will always wonder what color eyes she had. Her hair was curly and bright red. I wanted to cut off a tiny lock, but it felt like sacrilege, so I only have the memory.

You took the car seat out of the Audi without me knowing. I never had to ask. You quietly and reverently made things as comfortable at home as possible. You pulled at your hair, you couldn't sleep, and you obsessively researched a new espresso grinder because you needed something to distract you from the pain. We were broken, but broken together, and we immediately started building a new masterpiece.

Our healing journey has been a roller coaster. At times we've felt impenetrable, and other times there was a chasm between us. I frightened you in my desperation. You admitted you didn't know what to do, and you begged me to get help. We sobbed in each other's arms, and I got help.

We went to counseling together. We spent thousands of dollars learning how to strengthen our emotional bond to one another while we continued to grieve. We started wanting again. We started dreaming again. We had breakthroughs. We identified loops and patterns—our dance—that we get stuck in. And even though we still get stuck and smash and stub each other's toes, we continue to love and heal and grow. Let's never stop dancing.

When you and I conceived our daughter, we weren't "trying." We had no idea what was in store for our lives.

We loved Poppy with our whole hearts. Since her death, we have honored her time and time again, and she is a driving spiritual force in our marriage. Times have been really tough, honey. You and I have crawled through hell together. I didn't like hell, but at least you were there with me.

Our bond, this journey, takes work every day. We can't rest on our laurels if we want to have a joyful, adventurous, and fulfilling life together. You and I know that.

I adore you, Eli. You drive me crazy sometimes, but damn, you inspire me too. You get me thinking, you get me singing, you get me excited about the life we are building together. Thank you, darling from the bottom of my heart.

I've said it before, and I'll say it again:

Our love story is my favorite of all time.

ACKNOWLEDGMENTS

I am grateful to the many people who supported me over the six years it took me to write this book. I am constantly overwhelmed by the power of community, and I could not have finished this journey without the love, encouragement, and inspiration from mine.

First, I would like to express my love and gratitude to my beloved mother Louise Duke, my father Jim Duke, my sister Kellee Reid, and my brother Aaron Duke—I am so lucky to be in our family. Thank you to my extended family: John (Pop Pop) Muir, Shanna O'Brien, Michelle Duke, Joe Reid, Zoe and Josh Roddy, Eloisa and John Muir, and Alisa Van Dissen. I married into a fabulous bunch of folks.

To my amazing friends who walked me through some of my darkest days: Althea Cullen, Lucia Schaefer, Emma Milner, Suz Bisgaard, Keridwyn Deller, Jenna Bauer, Rebecca Sayre, Joy Shumaker, Kirsten Dahlquist, Dara Mclurkin, and Rachel Monnen. I love each of you so much! To the powerful tribe of amazing humans that continues to grow around me, there are so many of you who impact and bless my life—too many to list—if your name isn't here, I love you, too.

To my doctors, midwives, therapists, healers, and coaches, I couldn't have made it through without you. To my yoga teachers and spiritual mentors, your dedication to raising global consciousness and spreading love make a massive difference—thank you. A big thank you to my Facebook community. Since that first devastating post announcing Poppy's death in October 2015, you have liked, loved, and commented me into healing. You read my posts, you gave me hope, and you celebrated my reinvention. You reflected my courage and bravery, and you inspired me to continue following my heart and my dreams.

A sincere thank you to the mothers of children gone too soon, who had the courage to tell their stories before me and who inspired me to write mine: Elizabeth McCracken, Amelia Kathryn Barnes, Carol Cirulli Lanham, and Karla Helbert. There are many others out there doing incredible work and advocacy for the loss community. Keep it up! We are all making a difference.

A heartfelt thank you to Eric Koester of the Creator Institute for believing in my story and for making this experience fun. To the team at New Degree Press—thank you for saying yes. To Melody Delgado Lorbeer, my developmental editor, for helping me work through my creative blocks, to Kristy Elam, my acquiring editor, for her meaningful insights into my first draft, and to Michelle Pollack, my revisions editor, for helping me fine tune the manuscript. A special shout out to Kyra Ann Dawkins and John Saunders for their incredible energy and wisdom into the book writing and publishing process, and a high-five to Jeff Leisawitz, my writing coach who helped me embrace creative writing as a form of healing. You rock, Jeff.

A gigantic thank you to the beta readers who read my unpublished manuscript from start to finish: Stephanie Marshall, Jade Eby, Megan Dunn, Alisha Wielfaert, Teigan Johanna, Donna Meredith, Mary Lou Mirocha, Rachel Einbund, Megan Young, Jennifer Lindamood, Kelli Rippee, and Eli Muir—your feedback was priceless and transformed this book into what it is today.

To everyone who pre-ordered a copy of my book or made a financial contribution during my Indiegogo campaign, thank you for making this book a possibility and for believing in me.

Aaron Duke	Althea Cullen
Abbey Watt	Amana Faulkner
Abigail Newton	Amanda Diffenbaugh
Adam Quiney	Amelia Barnes
Aga Najarian	Amy Klosterman
Aika Patel	Angela Craven
Alexandra Goncalves	Anthea McLean
Alicia Mohler	Ariella Shuster
Alisa Van Dissen	Ashley Ross
Alisha Wielfaert	Audrey Lambert
Alisha Wiese	Barbara Burnett
Alison DeGregorio	Beverly Maxwell

Bobbie Cross

Brandee Slosar

Brice Canfield

Bruce Smith

Caitlin Pitchon

Camila Uliana de Gusmao

Carol Sue Janes

Cathy Thesis

Charmaine Bostwick

Cheryl Hunter

Chris Odom

Christina Sanini

Christina Winterbourne

Connie Duval

Corinne Xidos

Daniel Gero

Danielle Michaels

Danielle Ranney

Dara Mclurkin

Debra Diggs

Diana Dericks

Donna Kotulock

Donna Meredith

Elijah Farrell

Elizabeth Roots

Ella Erickson

Emily Loftiss

Emily Ward

Emma Milner

Eric Koester

Eric V Von Blon

Erica Johnson

Erin Wolfe

Ethan Carpenter

Eva Tallmadge

Faith Ireland

Gary Wortzel

George Banks, Jr.

Gordon Griggs

Gretchen Heying

Hans Kullberg

Heather Craig

Heather Davis

Heather Hokamp

Heather Ohannessian

Heidi Overmyer

Hiedi Star

Ivana Kenoi

Jade Kelly

James Mclurkin

Jamie Strayer

Jason Miller

Jason Strayer

Jeff Leisawitz

Jeffrey Shipley

Jen Reisinger

Jenna Bauer

Jennifer Baggs

Jennifer Burling

Jennifer Lindamood

Jennifer Tam

Jeremy Winters

Jessica Tartaro

Joanne Olsen

Jocelyn Nedved

Jody Davis

Jolynne Anderson

Joy Aardappel

Juli Lewis

Julie Mueller

Karen McNamara

Karen Summerville

Kate Suddes

Kathryn Foubister

Katie Chastain

Katie Hutt

Katie Mathias

Katie McKeehan Hart

Katie Sedgwick

Kaycie Wood

Keelin OBrien

Keith Wiley

Kellee Reid

Kelli Rippee

Kendra Martin

Kimberly Sandie

Kirsten Dahlquist

Krista Kauffman

Kristin Villani

LaNysha Adams, Ph.D.

Lara Clark

Laura Szabo-Kubitz

Leah Olson

Lesley Mondeaux

Leta Berkshire

Lisa LeDoux

Lisanna Smithhart

Liz Larsen

Loren West

Louisa Cranston

Louise Duke

Lucia Schaefer

Lynn Stowers

Maggie Mock

Malaine Schmid

Marie Miller

Marisa Mohr

Martha Early

Mary Carlson

Mary Lou Mirocha

Max Beery

Max Riggs

Megan Young

Meghan McGinn

Melissa Moize	Robert Duke
Melissa Willoughby	Robin West
Michael Halekakis	Rose Marie Robbins
Michelle Duke	Sadie (Adams) Potter
Mindy Longanecker Deranek	Sam Lamb
Molly Murphy	Sara Greengrass
Monica Knapp	Sarah Miller
Nancy McCaughey	Shanna Obrien
Naomi Hyland	Shannon Freeman
Natalie Herman	Shannon O'Keefe
Natalie Teravainen	Shannon Tipple-Leen
Nicole Duke	Shauna Louise Prince
Olaseni Bello	Shayla Malek
Pamela Nygaard	Sheri Hauser
Payton Lynch	Sherri Ames
Rachel Einbund	Sherry Hoffman
Rebecca Ramsey Nicolay	Sheryl Wilson
Rebecca Sayre	Shirley Senn
Rob Newsom	Shukria Pettie

Sidney Kreyenbuhl

Sky Earth Youngblood

Sonia Brown

Stephanie Marshall

Sue Ford

Sumit Basu

Summer Walker

Susan Groves

Suzanne Skjerdal Bisgaard

Tami Farber-Rogan

Teigan Johanna

Tiffany Scharn

Timothy Mangrum

Tina Ilvonen

Tonita Webb

Valeria Gheorghiu

Veronica Sturtevant

Vickie Adams

Zoe Roddy

Zoe Sonoda

Finally, thank you Poppy for choosing me. You are the essence of love. Thank you, Moxie, for being determined to be here and for shining so bright. Eli, I love, cherish, and thank you with all my heart.

APPENDIX

MY INSPIRATION

Brown, Brené. *Rising Strong: How the Ability to Reset Transforms the Way We Live, Love, Parent and Lead.* New York: Random House, 2015.

Hoyert, Donna L., PhD, and Elizabeth C.W. Gregory. "Cause of Fetal Death: Date From the Fetal Death Report, 2014". *National Vital Statistics Reports,* Volume 65, No. 7 of Issue 2016: 1-10. https://www.cdc.gov/ncbddd/stillbirth/facts.html#ref.

McCracken, Elizabeth. *An Exact Replica of a Figment of My Imagination.* New York: Little, Brown and Company, 2008.

Star Legacy Foundation, *About Stillbirth.* 2022. https://starlegacyfoundation.org/about-stillbirth/.

CHAPTER THREE: OUR CELEBRATION

Gibran, Kahlil. *The Prophet.* New York: Alfred A Knopf, 2000.

Reiner, Rob, dir. *The Princess Bride.* Los Angeles, CA: Act III Communications, 1987.

CHAPTER NINE: MY DREAM

Harms, Roger W. *The Mayo Clinic Guide to a Healthy Pregnancy*. New York: Harper Collins, 2004.

CHAPTER TEN: FRIENDSHIP AND FLOWERS

Ilse, Sherokee. *Empty Arms: Coping with Miscarriage, Stillbirth, and Infant Death*. Maple Plain: Wintergreen Press, 2002.

McCracken, Elizabeth. *An Exact Replica of a Figment of My Imagination*. New York: Little, Brown and Company, 2008.

Wolfelt, Alan D., PhD. *Healing Your Grieving Heart After Stillbirth, 100 Practical Ideas for Parents and Families*. Fort Collins: Companion Press, 2013.

CHAPTER THIRTEEN: OUR ROAD TRIP

Barnes, Amelia Kathryn (@ameliakyoga), "Welcome to the world, Lily Orysia. I can't believe this is real life. She is perfect and healthy and filling all of our hearts with so much love and joy. I'm the luckiest mom in the world." Instagram, November 21, 2015. https://www.instagram.com/p/-XM9gMkl1c/.

CHAPTER FOURTEEN: SHARING MY TRUTH

Brown, Brené. *Rising Strong: How the Ability to Reset Transforms the Way We Live, Love, Parent and Lead*. New York: Random House, 2015.

Helbert, Karla. *Yoga for Grief and Loss*. London and Philadelphia: Singing Dragon, 2016.